Helmut Felzmann

AF219532

No Death for Jesus

The Turin Shroud and the Resurrection of Christ

2021

**No Death for Jesus: The Turin Shroud and the Resurrection of
Christ**
ISBN 9783754311950
© 2021 Helmut Felzmann - All rights reserved

Printed and published by: BoD – Books on Demand, Norderstedt
Website of this book: www.shroud.info

Table of Contents

Preface

The Christian creed from the year 325 is rarely spoken today. Hardly anyone who has no problems with it: "Jesus Christ, God's only-begotten Son, conceived by the Holy Spirit, born of Virgin Mary, ...on the third day risen from the dead, ascended to heaven, he sits at the right hand of God."

Can that really have happened historically? Or are these just pious stories, out of date today. The fact is: someone who is really dead can no longer become alive. Either he wasn't really dead or he wasn't really alive after the crucifixion. Some theologians tend towards the second possibility: It would not be that important whether the grave was empty or full. The only important thing would be to believe in the Easter message, which gives hope and strength. Some voices become clearer: "Jesus died on the cross and his body was rotten in the grave as a result. That the rulers of this world and there power to bring death do not have the last word, that is the good news of faith.

"Wouldn't this message be the result of a denial of reality, desperate perseverance? In the Acts of the Apostles, Peter proclaimed to the religious leaders: "You crucified Jesus, but God raised him. We can testify to this!" Was he untruthful - or later the evangelist Luke? First Corinthians was written only 20 years after the crucifixion. Paul wrote that after Jesus was crucified, 500 brothers saw Jesus at the same time, some were still alive. Is it conceivable that the Jesus Movement could emerge if the core of the message was fake news?

What if God had worked a miracle and intervened in the physical process of things? It is one of the basic assumptions of science that everything in the universe happens according to fundamental rules. All processes are the effect of previous causes. The universe is not haunted! There are no spirits that act on matter from outside and set autonomous causes - apart perhaps from processes in the brain.

Science makes the world seem sober today. But it has also brought great progress to mankind. Shall we live in two worlds: scientifically for everyday life, and believing in miracles for religion? I don't think Jesus himself had a magical image of God. His Heavenly Father makes it rain on the just and the unjust. He acts through people and does not intervene directly in what is happening according to his taste - from the outside, so to speak.

There remains only one variant for solving the "Easter dilemma": He was not really dead. It can be assumed that the disciples **thought** their master was dead after the crucifixion and that everything was a miracle for them. Is it possible to survive a crucifixion? Mustn't the thrust of the lance have led to death? Jesus would have been the superhero par excellence, if he had visited his disciples afterwards as if nothing had happened. It seems that there is only a choice between the improbable (survival) and the impossible (resurrection).

In any case, something very special must have happened back then. Will the truth ever be found out? We weren't there. The eyewitnesses vehemently claimed that they had met Jesus in person after the crucifixion.

If the Turin shroud were genuine, it would have witnessed what went on in the grave. In addition to the old writings, there would then be an old cloth that could be questioned. It is almost as if Jesus himself were standing before us.

So let's go on an exciting journey to find out the truth about the resurrection.

The Turin Shroud – A Controversial Object

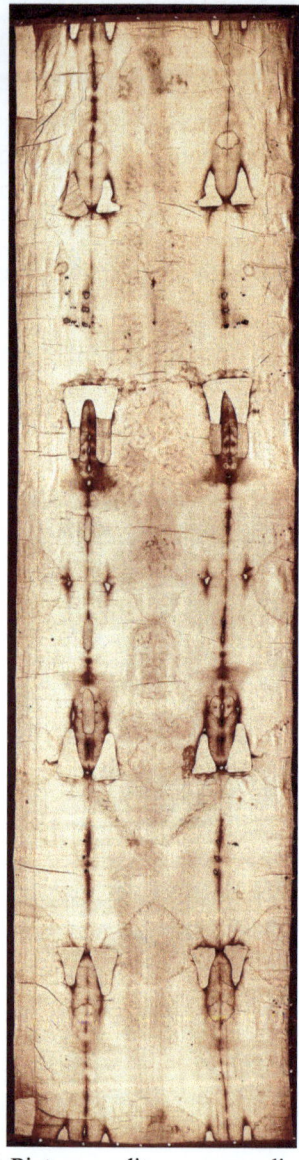

(1) Picture credits see appendix

Scarcely any historical object has been so intensively examined in so many disciplines as the Shroud of Turin. And scarcely any historical object has been so passionately debated.

The Shroud of Turin is a linen cloth measuring 436 centimeters in length by 110 centimeters in width on which the clear image of a crucified man can be seen, a man who was approximately thirty to forty years old and who stood approximately five feet ten inches tall (1.8 meters). The Shroud also bears various burn spots, as well as a series of bloodstains.

In 1978 the cloth was allowed to be examined by a team of scientists for 5 days (STURP project). The main question was how the image could have come about. The result was: We don't know. In no case can it be the work of an artist. If it was a natural process, energy must have leaked out of the body. From a corpse?

So, after all, a flash of energy during the resurrection that burned the image into the cloth? Did the picture come about in some inexplicable, supernatural way? Or was body heat the energy we are looking for? Then the man under the cloth couldn't have been dead. Whether the cloth is real and if so, which of the two options can be correct, is the real explosiveness of this cloth.

History of the Shroud and the Portrayal of Jesus

The indisputable history of the Shroud of Turin began in the year 1357[1]. In that year the widow of a French knight, Geoffroy de Charny, then in possession of the Shroud, decided out of financial desperation to display the Shroud publicly in the church of Lirey. The Shroud immediately attracted large groups of pilgrims and became so popular that the further history of the Shroud is recognized as being without gaps or doubts. How it had come into the possession of the de Charny family is, however, not known. Geoffrey's son later declared that his father had received the Shroud as a heartfelt gift. One hundred years later in 1452, a descendant of the de Charny family, for lack of an heir, bestowed the Shroud upon Louis of Savoy, head of the dynasty from which the kings of Italy later arose. In 1532 fire nearly destroyed the Shroud. The palace chapel of Chambery, in which the Shroud was kept at that time, burned to the ground. The Shroud itself lay folded together in a silver box, which melted from the heat on one corner so that the Shroud suffered serious damage. Very luckily, no portion of the Shroud was burned that had any significant part of the human image on it.

The Shroud remained in the possession of the House of Savoy until the year 1983, when the former king of Italy, Umberto, bequeathed it to the Vatican shortly before his death. Since 1578, however, it has remained in Turin.

On 15th of August 944 the "Image of Edessa" was transferred to the imperial capital of Constantinople after it was first rescued from the city of Edessa (now Sanliurfa in southeastern Anatolia) from the hands of the Arabs. In the festive calendar of the Orthodox Church this event is still commemorated each year on the 16th of August.

With the arrival of the image in Constantinople Gregory Referendarius, the Archdeacon of Sophia Haiga held a festive sermon, which remained completely preserved in a manuscript, and was only discovered in the Vatican archives as late as 1986.[2]

In the manuscript of his sermon, Gregory first tells the story of King Abgar of Edessa, then a small kingdom outside the Roman Empire. Abgar

---

1 The entire history of the Shroud is presented in great detail by Ian Wilson (1998) in his book, *The Blood and the Shroud*.

2 The Greek original text and a French translation was published in 1997 by André-Marie Dubarle in: Revue des Études Byzantines, No. 55, pp. 5-51 - Source quoted in this book: Mark Guscin, The Sermon of Gregory Referendarius, 2004, http://www.shroud.com/pdfs/guscin3.pdf

was terminally ill when he heard of the miracle healer Jesus in Judea. He sent a messenger with a letter to Jesus asking him to come to Edessa to cure him. But Jesus wrote him back that he must fulfill his mission and ascend to Him who has sent him. But that he would send him a disciple, who will heal him and bring life to him and to his family.

Here he quotes the Church-Father Eusebius, who has passed on the texts in the 4th Century ("Church History" 1.13). Eusebius says that he even traveled to Edessa, has "taken the original manuscripts from the archives [in Edessa] and has literally translated them from the Syriac language".

Gregory continues that he has also traveled with companions to Edessa searching for manuscripts, which would report additional acts of Abgar. And indeed they have found a greater number of manuscripts in the Syriac language, which he has copied in parts and translated into the Greek language. He quotes: King Abgar said to Thaddaios, "tell me how the image on the linen that cured me was made, since I can see it was not produced with ordinary paint, and explain its special strength, since when I saw it unfolded on your face I was cured of my illness and got up from my bed, and I felt the strength that I had in my body when I was in my prime".

Thaddaios replied, the image would have been created in the Garden of Gethsemane, where Jesus has made it miraculously out of his sweat and his blood. Jesus would have given it to Thomas first, who handed it over to Thaddaios, who then has brought it to Edessa. All this did he, Gregory, find in the manuscripts.

Gregory then explains why the image can not be a work of art: *"A Painting establishes a complete form with various beautiful colours, representing the cheeks with a blooming red, the encircling of the lips with red, it paints the beard with flowery gold, the eyebrow with shining black, the whole eye in beautiful colours, the ears and nose in a different way... This reflection, however – let everyone be inspired with the explanation – has been imprinted only by the sweat from the face of the originator of life ... Both are highly instructive – blood and water there, here sweat and image ... The source of living water can be seen and it gives us water, showing us that the origin of the image made by sweat is in fact of the same nature as the origin of that which makes the liquid flow from the side."*

(2) Arrival of the Mandylion in Constantinople on August 15, 944 (miniature, 11th century)

(3) The messenger hands over to King Abgar the cloth with the image (icon, 10th century)

In another text from Constantinople, ascribed to the emperor Constantine VII and also from 944[3], it is reported about this great event, too, the image from Edessa coming to Constantinople. It repeats the story of Abgar but then reports that not much later (still in the first century) Abgar's grandson (Manu VI) reverted to paganism and the cloth was in great danger. The bishop of the city therefore brought the cloth together with an oil lamp to a safe place: a niche near a gate in the city wall. In front of the cloth, a ceramic plate was placed which carried an identical copy of the miraculous image. The bishop *"then sealed the surface with gypsum and baked bricks finishing the wall off on the same level."* [4]

The history of the Abgar image continued like this: During a flood parts of the city walls of Edessa were destroyed. More destruction came during the siege of the city by the Turks. The city wall had to be repaired. In the year 525 during the reconstruction-work the cloth was rediscovered.[5] By at least 544 the image was worshiped as the icon of the Redeemer not made by hands (Acheiropoieton). The image was first mentioned by the historian Evagrius Scholasticus, who wrote in his Ecclesiastical History of 594 in connection with the siege by the Persians in 544: *"When they were completely at a loss, they brought the image created by God, not made by human hands, which Christ, our God, has sent to Abgar, after he wanted to see him."*

In the "Acts of Thaddaios " (6th century) is reported: *"During the siege the bishop of the city had a vision in which the place in the city wall was shown to him, where the cloth resided. In the morning the bishop went to the place, praying and relying on the clear vision, examined it and found the divine image untouched and intact, together with the lamp, which did not extinguish during so many years. On a brick, which has been put before the lamp for protection there was another image of the likeness, which is kept in Edessa until today."*[6]

3 Daniel C. Scavone, Acheiropoietos Jesus Images in Constantinople: the Documentary Evidence, 2006, Narratio de Imagine Edessena 944, http://www.shroud-story.com/scavone/scavone.doc
4 Marc Gustin, The Image of Edessa, „The Narratio de Imagine Edessena", S. 33 quoted from Philip E. Dayvault, Face of the God-man, 2011, http://www.k-eramion502.com/article-link
5 Report from the byzantine historian Prokop from Caesare
6 Illert, Thaddäusakten, quoted from http://www.heiliges-antlitz.de/Dokumente/Volto-Mandylion_vGenua.pdf

In Edessa the cloth was folded in a way that only the face was visible. Therefore the fact that it was a complete shroud gradually was forgotten. Only when it was first examined in Constantinople in 944, it was discovered that the cloth was a burial shroud on which the entire body is visible.

When former FBI agent Philip Dayvault 2002 in search of ancient oil lamps, carried out an investigation in the Museum of Sanliurfa (formerly Edessa), a brick slab was shown to him with a mosaic of Jesus. The Muslim museum director told him that it would be the most valuable piece of the museum and would show Isa (the word for Jesus in Islam). Dayvault therefore called it "ISA-Tile".[7] The director told him that it had come into the possession of the museum 1972, from someone who had carved it out of a wall. Nothing more was known.

The mosaic was still part of a stone. Dayvault photographed the stone from different perspectives and started to investigate in the ruins of the ancient city walls. And indeed he succeeded at the western city gate: he was able to clearly identify a complementary spot in the wall.

The story with photo can be found on the Internet at www.keramion502.com The mosaic is almost identical to one of the first portraits of Christ in Rome (Santa Costanza, middle of the 4th century). The similarity is indeed striking: the face, the strands of hair, even the blood stains on the nose and lips match with the ISA-Tile.

There is an excellent slide presentation on the Internet on the subject of how the Turin shroud shaped the portrayal of Jesus in history[8].

Portrayals of Jesus in ancient Rome

In the catacombs in Rome many portrayals of Jesus from the first centuries have survived. Until the third century there were only symbolic representations, like the beardless shepherd, which have little in common with portrayals of Jesus as we know them today.

The first portrayals of Jesus that correspond to the familiar image of Christ did not appear until the time of Emperor Constantine.

---

7 The story can be found at: http://www.keramion502.com/article-link

8 Emanuela Marinelli: The Shroud and the Iconography of Christ
  www.shroud.com/pdfs/stlemarinellippt.pdf

(4) Mosaic of Christ: Church Santa Costanza (Rome, mid-4th century)

5) Jesus as Good Shepherd

(6) Catacombs of Marcellinus and Paul (second half of the 4th century)

(7) Santa Putenziana (Rome 315 AD). Considered the oldest mosaic image of Jesus of which the age is known.

The Lateran basilica was built by Constantine in 312-314. The church was severely damaged several times by earthquakes and fire. Nevertheless, according to tradition, it is considered the oldest mosaic image of Christ as it was restored repeatedly during all the repairs at the original location. "When the apse was restored about 100 years ago, under Pope Leo XIII., it was found that the Christ-mosaic is mounted within a stone-cartridge which is anchored in the masonry with iron bands. This strongly suggests that it is still essentially the original image."[9]

What caused this sudden change? Why so late in the 4th century? Where does the similarity to the Jesus mosaic in Edessa come from? At the time when these images were made, the ISA mosaic and the cloth were walled and forgotten in the citadel of Edessa at the end of the empire. Therefore the mosaic could not have been in Rome at this time. It can only be speculated how this information originally came to Rome. The similarity between the ISA mosaic and the Jesus portraits of Constantine do suggest such an exchange of information.

The tale of Abgar is also mentioned in the Syriac Doctrina Addai.[10] In addition it is reported that the archivist and court painter of Abgar, Hannan, who knew Jesus personally: "*took and painted a likeness of Jesus with choice paints, and brought with him to Abgar the king, his master. And when Abgar the king saw the likeness, he received it with great joy, and placed it with great honor in one of his palatial houses.*"

Of course, in these stories and legends not every word can be considered as historically true. Nevertheless, it seems reasonable to ascribe a historical core and to assume that in Edessa there was indeed knowledge of what the historical Jesus looked like and that this knowledge was preserved in the form of portraits and copies. .

Eusebius was bishop of Caesarea in Palestine from 313. He is regarded as a Father of the Church and founder of the History of the Church. He was present at the Council of Nicaea in person and signed the results of the council, albeit with reservations.

After the death of Constantine, he wrote the book "The Life of Constantine", a tendentious panegyric on the emperor. Prof. Friedrich Vittinghoff, professor of ancient history, calls Eusebius "court bishop of Constantine".[11] Caeserea was only 500 miles away from Edessa. Eusebius writes that he had personally traveled to Edessa and had done research in the archives there. Is

---

9 Werner Bulst, Betrug am Grabtuch - Der manipulierte Carbontest, 1990, p. 54
www.shroud.info/bulst.pdf (in German)

10 G. Phillips, The Doctrine of Addai the Apostle, London 1876,
http://www.tertullian.org/fathers/addai_2_text.htm

11 Vittinghoff, Eusebius als Verfasser der „Vita Constantini", Festschrift,
http://www.rhm.uni-koeln.de/096/Vittinghoff.pdf

it unreasonable to assume that he brought from Edessa examples showing the appearance of the historical Jesus and disseminated it via his channels?

Unfortunately, hardly any images of Jesus have been preserved on the territory of the Byzantine Empire dating before the 10th Century as during the iconoclastic controversy the emperors ordered that all representations of Jesus were to be removed from churches and be destroyed.

The equalization of the depiction of Jesus in the 6th Century

It is noticeable that the depictions of Jesus from the time of Constantine onward, are similar, but differ in details. There were also depictions of Jesus, which diverged completely from the common Jesus type.

This changes around the middle of the 6th century with the rediscovery of the shroud cloth, when its image quickly became the standard for representations of Jesus because it was venerated as "the true face of Jesus." There are countless icons bearing a copy of the Mandylion in various eastern churches.

Until World War I the Mandylion even was carried in battles as a sign of divine protection.

(8) Russian troops with the Mandylion as their battle standard Imperial War Museum, London

Interesting is the transformation of mosaics of Christ in Ravenna. This city experienced its most fruitful period in the fifth and sixth centuries,

14

and it has mosaics that were produced in the decades just before and after the rediscovery of the cloth. Here are two typical examples:

(9) Mosaic in Ravenna before 544...   (10) ... and after 544 (San Vitale)

(11) Jesus Pantocrator

St. Catherine's Monastery, Sinai, ca. 550, compared with the face of the shroud

Professor Whanger has also discovered in the Jesus Pantocrator icon representations of flowers in the same places as on the Shroud of Turin.[12]

Eastern Roman emperors liked to stamp the "not hand-made image of the Redeemer" on their coins.[13]

(12) Coin of Emperor Justinian (7th century) next to the face of the shroud

Yet is the cloth of Edessa, and later of Constantinople, the same as the Shroud of Turin? There exists an interesting piece of evidence connecting them. In the National Library of Budapest is preserved a parchment manuscript from the second half of the twelfth century called the *Codex Pray Manuscript*. This contains a report about a visit to Constantinople by a Hungarian mission in the year 1150.

---

12 Marry and Alan Whanger, The Shroud of Turin - An Adventure of Discovery, 1998 p. 35

13 See the standard work: Giulio Fanti, Byzantine Coins Influenced by the Shroud of Christ, 2021

A miniature from the manuscript shows the placement of Jesus' body into its final resting place (upper portion of picture). On the hands of Jesus only four fingers can be seen. This is exceptional in medieval representations of the burial, as is the nakedness of the body. Interestingly, both correspond exactly to the image on the Turin Shroud. On the lower portion of the picture, a representation of the Shroud itself can be seen. This particular picture is most interesting for the four L-shaped dots (circled) shown. They are older holes from previous fire damage and still visible on the shroud today in this precise configuration and at this precise place on the Shroud of Turin.

Codex Pray Manuscript of 1192 National Széchényi Library Budapest - Courtesy of Barrie Schwortz

Another link between the Shroud of Constantinople and the Shroud of Turin is the Gero-cross at the Cathedral of Cologne. It is the oldest preserved large crucifix in the European region north of the Alps. Created during the Ottonian dynasty at the end of the tenth century, it is reputed to be one of the first monument sculptures of the Middle Ages. In the history of occidental iconography, it represents a change of the presentation of the Christ, who until then was portrayed heroically and victoriously in an upright position. The Gerocross for the first time depicted the Christ as human and suffering. The sculpture was the prototype for many subsequent representations of Jesus on the cross in the Middle Ages.

In 1976, a dendrochronological procedure was performed on the cross.[14] Results showed that the oak from which the cross was made must have been cut down shortly after 965. Pastor Wilhelm Jordan investigated the history of the crucifix, referring to the *Chronicles of Thietmar of Merseburg*, written by a contemporary of Gero between 1012 and 1018.[15] The *Chronicles* reported the following:

---

14 Through the counting of the tree rings, which for climatic reasons can vary in thickness, the exact age of a tree can be determined at the time of felling.

- Archbishop Gero of Cologne was sent to Constantinople by the German emperor Otto I in 971 to find a bride for his son, Prince Otto. When negotiations with regard to Thoephanu, the niece of the Bycantine emperor, were completed, Gero wanted to visit the town, especially the famous Mandylion.

- Theophanu not only told him its history but arranged to have a parchment of the Mandylion made, which Gero took back with him to Cologne. There Prince Otto and Theophanu married in 972.

- Gero died in 976. Theophanu arranged to have a wooden cross made in the likeness of the image of the body depicted on the parchment made at Mandylion. The new cross was then erected near Gero's grave in the church.

This stone Mandylion can be found near the templar chapel "Sainte-Marie du Menez Hom," South Brittany (France) Courtesy Francois Gazay © 2001 - photo André Bruscq
http://www.cirac.org/Mandylion.pdf

Gero-cross (Cologne cathedral)

---

15 Jordan, Wilhelm: Das Gerokreuz in Kőln und das Turiner Grablinnen, Queckenberg, 1989. Information can be found in Barbara M. Sullivan's "The Shroud of Turin: The Model or Template of Sculptures, 10th–14th Centuries," *Holy Shroud Guild Newsletter*, January 2002.

Not only does the head of the Gerocross match the face on the Shroud of Turin (Shroud of Constantinople), but the closed thumbs match those on the shroud, as well, which is remarkable. In almost all illustrations of the crucifixion, the thumb is far outstretched. A depiction of the thumb in this unnatural position —which mirrors that of the image on the Turin Shroud —is exceptional.

Remaining after the sack of Constantinople

The Shroud did not remain long in Constantinople. The Fourth Crusade led the Crusaders not to Palestine as before. On April 13, 1204, the Crusaders conquered and plundered Constantinople. The city never fully recovered from that siege. The Shroud also disappeared at that time.

The Shroud then lay in the shadows of history for approximately 150 years. When in 1306 the French king, Philip the Handsome, disbanded the Order of the Knights Templars, which had become too powerful for his taste, a story surfaced in the records of the interrogations of the Templars about a certain "idol" that had the form of a man's head with a big beard and had great meaning in the mystery cults of the Templars.

The Templars, however, preserved their secret even during their painful interrogations, never surrendering the "idol." Those who knew the secret were all executed. The gap in the Shroud record closed with its public exhibition in Lirey (1357) by the widow of the knight Geoffroy de Charny.

(14) Pilgrim's medal from Lirey (1357). It contains all the details of the Turin Shroud: nudity of the body, traces of the torture, bloodstains ...

Under the Shroud Laid a Real Crucified Man

Modern research on the Shroud was inspired by an event on May 28, 1898. The Turin lawyer Secondo Pia, a reputable amateur photographer, was invited to photograph the Shroud of Turin for the first time.

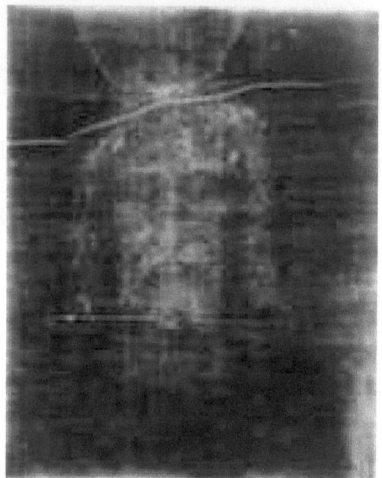

First photograph of the face ot the Turin Shroud (Pia 1898)

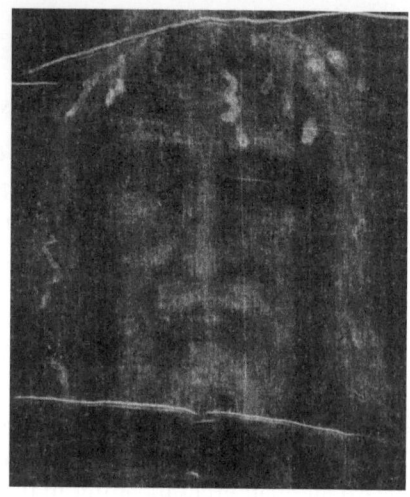

Enrie 1931

When Secondo Pia removed the photographic plate from the developing liquid and looked at it, he almost dropped it from sheer excitement. He recognized instantly that the image on the Turin Shroud actually represented a kind of negative. He saw in his photographic negative a positive image. While the eyes appear open on the original, for example, one could now see clearly that they are closed.

The Shroud has been venerated for a long time as the original burial shroud of Jesus Christ. Could it be true that the only known "photograph" prior to the nineteenth century just happens to show the crucified Jesus?

In 1978 the former king of Italy, Umberto, the owner of the Shroud at the time, gave permission for an intensive examination. Forty scientists and other experts had five days to examine the Shroud directly, using many scientific methods. Altogether more than 150,000 working days were invested in the entire project by the time the results were published in 1981. The Shroud even has its own scientific field: Sindology, whose members from many fields devote themselves to this one object.

Here are the most important results:

Medical examiners say that the image is clearly that of a brutally tortured, real man. There is no anatomical detail that does not fit that conclusion. An example makes this clear. In virtually all of the representations of the crucifixion of Jesus in history, the nails are shown as driven through the palms of his hands. In the 1930s, the chief surgeon of St. Josephs-Hospital in Paris, Pierre Barbet, experimented with amputated arms, with the result that a body weight of only eighty-eight pounds would cause the nailed flesh of the palms to give way and rip through, causing the body to drop.[16] However, nails would successfully hold up the body weight if driven through the base of the hands by the wrists, through the so-called "space of Destot," as the Shroud image indeed shows. At this spot, the bones of the bottom of the hand surround a tiny hole, through which a thick nail can nevertheless be forced. The danger of the hand ripping apart under the body weight is thus eliminated. Virtually all artistic representations of the crucifixion are, therefore, historically incorrect. Moreover, an important nerve, the median nerve, is injured by driving the nail through this space. This leads to unbearable pain and at the same time causes the thumb to be drawn in toward the palm of the hand automatically. This is the reason why only the fingers are seen on the image but no thumb, as the miniature manuscript illustration from Budapest clearly shows.

The bloodstains consist of real human blood of type AB.[17]

Painters state that there are no traces of brushstrokes on the Shroud. Tiny amounts of coloring or pigments have been shown to be on the Shroud, but only because copies of the Shroud were repeatedly painted, and the copies were then pressed against the original as a form of validation. Such tiny particles of paint are, moreover, spread over the entire Shroud, not only on the areas showing the human image. By no means do these particles represent the substance from which the image itself is made. The substance appears as a yellowish, brownish layer on the uppermost fibers of the Shroud, as if it had been singed or scorched.

Textile experts say that the style of weaving seen in the Shroud fabric is one that was used in the ancient Middle East.

---

16 Barbet P., *Die Passion Christi in der Sicht des Chirurgen*, 1953.

17 Heller und Adler, "A Chemical Investigation of the Shroud of Turin," *Canadian Society for Forensic Science Journal*, 14.3, 1981.

On the Shroud, pollen from many different plants has been found. The criminologist Max Frei found traces of fifty-nine different plants. Of those, forty-four grow in the area around Jerusalem, and fourteen grow exclusively in Jerusalem. But also the assumed trail of the Shroud is confirmed by pollen analysis: eighteen types of the plants grow in the steppe area of Anatolia, of which six are found exclusively in the area of Edessa (today Urfa). Fourteen of the other plant types grow in the area of Istanbul, and seventeen grow in Western Europe.[18]

Prof. Whanger claims to have found even more remarkable images on the Shroud. They are objects such as an amulet, a Roman spear, a pair of primitive pliers, a hammer, a nail, and a whip. Moreover, they all match the sizes and shapes of real objects that were used in first-century Palestine. It was a Jewish custom to bury a dead person with every object that bore some of that person's blood on it.[19]

Rev. Francis Filas, S.J., and Michael Marx, a specialist in classical coins, examined the area of the right eye on the body image and discovered a pattern that appears as the letters UCAI, a portion of the inscription TIBERIOUCAISAROS, which is known to appear on ancient Roman coins minted during the reign of the Emperor Tiberius. They also found a pattern that matches a curved staff (lituus). Filas therefore concluded that it was a coin of the type *lituus lepton*, which Pontius Pilate minted in Judaea between AD 29 and 32. Over the left eye, Filas believed to have found a joulia lepton coin, which was minted in the year 29 to honor the wife of Tiberius, Julia. Prof. Whanger, who undertook similar coin studies, came to the same conclusion.[20] These results are debated within the field however. Skeptics state that the patterns could be simply random shapes and noises only interpreted as letters.

The degree of coloration (gray scale) of the image depends directly on the distance that the Shroud was from the body. In the 1970s a computer program analyzed a photograph of the image for any three dimensional qualities it might have. The findings were impressively realistic. The higher and lower areas on the face and the rest of the body are clear. This

18 Frei M., *Il passato della Sindone alla luce della Palinologia, Sindone e Scienza*, 1978.

19 Michael Hesemann, *Die stummen Zeugen von Golgatha. Die faszinierende Geschichte der Passionsreliquien Christi*, 2000.

20 Oswald Scheuermann, *Das Tuch – Neueste Forschungsergebnisse zum Turiner Grabtuch*, 1982. Images can be seen at_
_www.theholyshroud.net/Coins.htm

breathtaking result is probably the best evidence that the image is no mere painting.[21]

Three-dimensional image of the wounded face of the man in the Shroud, according to computer analysis.

Courtesy G. Tamborelli and N. Balossinio

The formation of the image itself remained a riddle for science for a long time, as was also expressed in the final report of the STURP project:

We can conclude for now that the Shroud image is that of a real human form of a scourged, crucified man. It is not the product of an artist. The blood stains are composed of hemoglobin and also give a positive test for serum albumin. The image is an ongoing mystery and until further chemical studies are made, perhaps by this group of scientists, or perhaps by some scientists in the future, the problem remains unsolved.[22]

21 Jackson, Jumper, Ercoline, *Three Dimensional Characteristics of the Shroud Image.*, Proceedings of the IEEE International Conference on Cybernetics and Society, 1982, 559–75.

22 See http://www.shroud.com/78conclu.htm

23

The Shroud Cannot Be a Forgery

The hypothesis that the Shroud might be a forgery has received much attention since the announcement of the results of the carbon 14 test in 1988.[23] If one assumes that the Shroud was first created in the Middle Ages, it can only be a fake. The question is however, how an artist could have made this "fake-masterpiece"? Several methods have been proposed by skeptics in order to proof how easy it is to fake such an image. Of course with some skill the optical appearance of the image can be somehow mirrored. But a forger would have to reproduce **all** the characteristics of the shroud especially the chemical and anatomical ones.

Pollen grains from plants that only grow in the Jerusalem area have been found on the Shroud. These types of pollen were also the most frequently found on the Shroud, not pollen from plants that grow in France or Italy, where the Shroud has been kept uninterruptedly since the thirteenth century.

On the basis of the images of plant parts found on the Shroud, plants, especially flowers, must have been laid on the body during the burial— plants that only grow in the area around Jerusalem. A forger would have had to travel to Palestine in order either to place such plants on the Shroud, or else "depict" these plants somehow, a difficult project at that time because the area in question was under Muslim rule. And why should a forger have gone to such lengths? These plant images were discovered and identified on the Shroud in the twentieth century.

The image on the Shroud provides a sort of photographic negative that contains three-dimensional information, which by means of a computer program can be enhanced to reveal a relief-like representation. Such a process of three-dimensional enhancement, however, does not work with paintings or photographs.

Meanwhile, the historical trail of the Shroud from before the thirteenth century has been documented. Already in the Eastern Roman Empire it played a major role: the unified representation of the face of Jesus on the icons of the East goes back to the Shroud image.

Medical examiners who have studied the Shroud and have made statements about it stand unified in their findings that it is an authentic image

---

23 The Shroud was subject to a carbon 14 testing in 1988, and the results dated the Shroud to the Middle Ages. This test will be discussed later.

of a crucified man. In the more than one hundred-year history of research on the Shroud, no anatomic detail has been found on it that is not correct, despite constant searching for evidence of fakery.

Here are the most important hypotheses of forgery for the Shroud:

Painting. There are no significant traces of painting, nor application of paint, nor colored surfaces. The yellowish layer that makes the image appears under a microscope as a very thin chemical coating on the topmost fibers. The fibers themselves were not altered or saturated with any coloring.

Hot bronze surface relief. In this case, all fibers would be darker, not only individual ones on the surface of the fabric. The fibers are coated all around with a chemical coating. Had this coating been formed by heat, the interior of the fibers would also have been affected. Otherwise, the opposite side of the fibers would not have been discolored by that heat. Also, reflected light would show another spectrum in ultraviolet photographs. There is wide consensus today among Sindologists that the image must have been caused by a low-temperature process (air/body temperature).

There are thus no known methods of forgery by means of which all characteristics of the Shroud could have been artificially created. The Shroud contains anatomical details that are far beyond what was known in the Middle Ages. Even relatively insignificant details fit exactly with the authenticity of the Shroud and its image. For example, in the area of the feet considerable traces of street dust have been discovered. What medieval artist would have gone to such lengths to make his artificial relic so realistic? At the time, a pretty story was sufficient for an old bone of any alleged saint to be set in gold and venerated.

The Shroud is simply too good to be a forgery. Many highly qualified medical examiners have occupied themselves with the Shroud and did not doubt that they were studying the genuine image of a crucified man. We can be confident that these scientists were in a position to distinguish a genuine image from medieval "art work." It is precisely the accuracy of all medical and anatomical details that definitively excludes the possibility of forgery. A crucified man must once have lain under the Shroud, whose body, by whatever process, projected its image permanently onto the Shroud.

It is simply absurd to assume that a medieval person, however inventive he or she may have been, could deceive a series of high-ranking scientists of the twentieth and now twenty-first centuries. There is no tradition in medieval art that could have produced the Shroud or similar "works." The Shroud of Turin is absolutely unique. There is no other object in human history that even approaches comparison with the image on the Shroud.

If you are still not convinced of the authenticity of the Shroud, I would now like to introduce you to quite another, even revolutionary discovery on the Shroud, which conclusively eliminates the possibility of forgery.

A Living Man among the Dead

Signs of life are surely the last thing that one would expect to find on a burial shroud. Who would suspect a living person among the dead? Moreover, the circumstances would all indicate that the man under the Shroud of Turin must have been dead: the brutal mistreatment, the crucifixion, and the fact that a burial was indeed carried out. No one could survive these serious wounds. Even if the whipping and the crucifixion had not led to death, the lance thrust - directly into the heart, as some believe - must at last have led to death. And, indeed, a Roman execution squad cannot be deceived. It is simply absurd to assume that this man made fools of almost all witnesses to his crucifixion and his burial - a Houdini escape in the history of crucifixions, so to speak.

Around 1950 a certain Hans Naber in post-war Germany expressed the belief that Jesus did not die on the cross. Naber based this belief on a direct message from Jesus Christ to himself, as well as on observations of the Turin Shroud. He claimed too much blood was present on the Shroud, whereas corpses no longer bleed—or at least the large quantity of blood on the shroud does not correspond to the blood emissions from a typical corpse. Naber was very active and published a series of books. He was, however, strongly attacked and even sentenced to two years in prison for fraud. Both the German media and the church authorities, simply ignored him. Nevertheless, in 1969 the Turinese Cardinal Pellegrino convened a commission of experts, unnoticed by the public, to test Naber's hypothesis with the Shroud at hand. The result was as expected: "The Man under the Shroud had really been dead, and Naber is wrong with his claim."[24] But the idea had been launched into the modern world, and later authors came to the same conclusion.[25]

What is it about this idea that the man on the Shroud was still alive in his tomb and that evidence from the Shroud confirms this?

Basically, this question of life or death can be answered only by developing two scenarios. First, what would be expected if the man were dead, and second, what if the man were still alive? Important are the bloodstains, traces of rigor mortis, as well as whether this basic assumption can

---

24 The whole story is told at http://www.kroi.de/naber3.htm

25 Holger Kersten: *Jesus Lived in India*, 1983; *The Jesus Conspiracy*, 1992; Rodney Hoare, *The Turin Shroud Is genuine*, 1984/94; Helmut Felzmann, *Revolution im Christentum*, 2002; und Gerhard Kuhnke, *Rom und das Grabtuch*, 2004.

explain the forming of the image on the shroud. Naturally, one must take into consideration the "entire picture" when conclusively deciding the validity of any hypothesis, as details leave some room open for interpretation, and one can always speculate about circumstances that would explain individual aspects of the Shroud, by which more than one scenario becomes possible.

Bloodstains

It was found that blood flowed out of at least twenty-eight wounds while the man was in the tomb. Most of the blood came out of the side wound, yet a considerable amount of blood also flowed out of the nail wounds in the hands and feet, as well as the thorn wounds on the back of the head. Precisely this picture is to be expected if the body were still alive. If this blood flow had not occurred, it would be a certain indication that a corpse must have lain upon the Shroud. But could it also be possible that so much blood flowed out of a corpse?

Of course, corpses can also "bleed" out of large wounds on the lower part of the body due to gravity. During transport of a corpse, the emission of blood is possible if pressure occurs in areas containing blood.

Looking very carefully at the individual bloodstains on the Shroud, one must differentiate the possible from the impossible. The late Prof. Wolfgang Bonte, former head of the Forensic Medicine Institute at the University of Dusseldorf and president of the International Organization of Forensic Scientists (IAFS) attempted to answer this question in the 1990s.[26]

First consider the bleeding from the wound on the side (the lance thrust wound). The lower back must have lain in a puddle of blood because bloodstains spread right and left six to eight inches beyond the area covered by the image of the body.

Karl Herbst, a retired Catholic priest, wrote Professor Bonte with this information without revealing to him that the Turin Shroud was involved, in order that Bonte's judgment would not be prejudiced. Bonte wrote back to Herbst that, according to this description, the opening of the wound on the right front chest wall was placed rather precisely on the highest point on the body. A spontaneous post-mortem blood flow was

---

26 Described in detail including the expert opinion of Prof. Bonte in Karl Herbst, *Kriminalfall Golgatha*, p. 97ff. and also Kuhnke, p. 75ff.

impossible because the blood level in the wound would have to have been lower than the opening of the wound. In such a case, no blood can flow out of a corpse.

On the contrary, a blood flow in the proportions described by you, including the direction of the flow, would agree with the idea that the individual involved was still alive at this time . . . this applies especially then, when larger arterial vessels are opened and when the blood pressure produces the necessary pressure against gravity for the blood to leave the body.[27]

Herbst then revealed to Bonte that the matter involved was the Shroud of Turin and provided photographs and specialist literature for him in which the blood flows on the Shroud had been described in connection with a corpse. Above all, Herbst made Bonte aware of the argumentation of the Italian medical examiner Prof. Bollone, who had declared that "*the cause* [of the exit of blood on the shroud] *is to be sought in the manipulation of the corpse during the burial procedures.*" Professor Bonte, however, maintained his opinion and wrote back to Herbst: *I will not repeat my earlier arguments. In my opinion, everything speaks to the fact that the blood circulation activity had not yet ended. Obviously I agree with Prof. Bollone that in the course of the transport of a corpse blood can flow almost passively out of such a stab wound to the chest. Yet one has to pose the question of whether the burial shroud was wrapped around the corpse already at the beginning of the transport. I believe that in this case no so-called statically stain-pattern would have been formed, which without exception permitted a direct, topographical assignment to a lying body. I would then far more have expected numerous traces of smears, whose locations would have been strewn more coincidental and irregularly. The pattern that is in fact recognizable indicates, in my opinion, that the person involved was only wrapped in the shroud during the placement in his grave, and indeed very probably in the form that at first the body was bedded on the shroud and the shroud's other half was then drawn over the body. I cannot imagine that during this placement a considerable quantity of blood could have flowed out passively.*[28]

As further evidence for a dead body, it is often said that serum areas would indicate post-mortem blood. To this claim, Professor Bonte wrote: *In my opinion, a great deal of unqualified comments has been said about another phenomenon. I mean the differentiation between the actual bloodstains and the serum areas that surround them, and which are seen as proof of corpse blood. In general one can say that corpse blood does*

27 Herbst, p. 98.
28 Herbst, p. 99. own translation

not differ from the blood of a living person at least in the first phase after death. In earlier times corpse blood was used for purposes of transfusion in great quantities. But if one cannot be differentiated from the other, it can not be concluded from any results that the one or the other type of blood is involved. It is correct that with bleeding in the chest cavity a re-duction of blood corpuscles can result, and quasi serum can develop. If such an emulsion is brought to flow out by a passive movement of the body, it is possible that indeed serum can escape first. This blood corpus-cle lowering can begin, depending on the circumstances, already during life. Having only the end result it can not be concluded whether the indi-vidual involved was already dead or still alive. I am therefore of the con-viction that nothing at all can be determined from this particular evi-dence, that is, neither that it must have been corpse blood nor that it was the blood of a still living person.[29]

The Shroud was folded double under the feet, and both layers were soaked through with **fresh** blood from the nail wound. This blood even soaked the opposite side of the Shroud, as the top half of the shroud was wrapped around the feet (see the illustrations).[30] So much blood flowed out of the soles of the feet that a total of three Shroud layers were soaked. That seems impossible in the case of a dead body with no circulation of its blood.

---

29 Herbst, p. 100.
30 Herbst, p. 90.

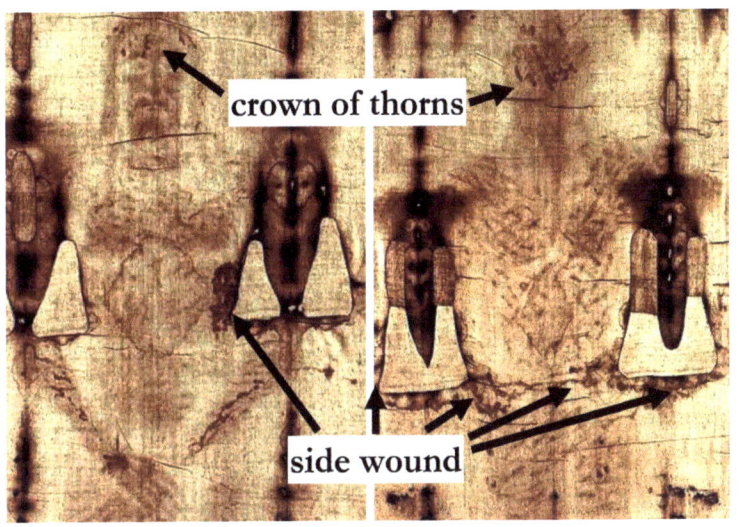

Bloodstains from the crown of thorns and from the side wound (Enrie)

top half of the cloth

blood-
stains

bottom half of the cloth

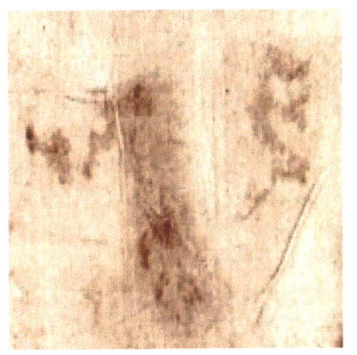

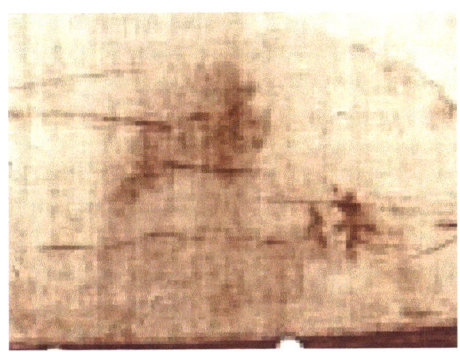

Bloodstains from nail wounds in the   ... and top half of the cloth
feet - bottom half ...

An interesting piece of evidence is also presented by the bloodstains in the nail wound of the right hand. There are two longer, narrow, clearly distinct courses of blood (called "Blutbahn" in the image), which together form an angle of about twenty-two degrees. Furthermore, there is a third, rather wide and almost round flow of blood roughly at a right angle to the other two that is not clearly delimited and must have formed when the body was in a horizontal position.

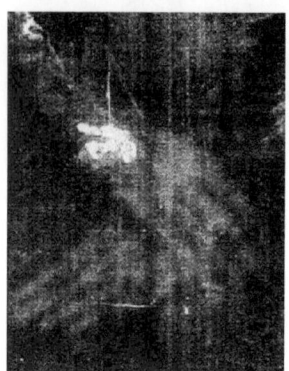 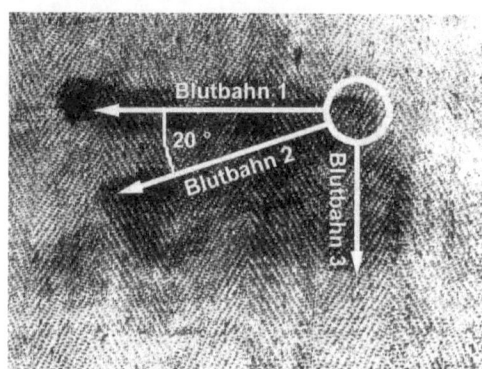

Blood flows on the right hand ©Enrie, Kersten, and Gruber

In experiments, imitation blood flows were painted on the arms of a volunteer, who was then hanged on a cross. It was apparent: one of the two longer blood flows must have been formed when the body hung upright on the cross (Blutbahn (bloodflow) 2). The other blood flow must have been formed after the crucified man lost consciousness and fell to one side (Blutbahn 1). Looking carefully, one can see that blood flow 1 is narrower than blood flow 2 and is also straight. This can be explained by the fact that the body hung motionless on the cross at the time it formed, while with blood flow 2 the blood ran irregularly down the arm due to the movement of the body.

The alternative interpretation, that the two blood flows arose when the crucified man occasionally changed his position in order to achieve some minor comfort, can be excluded, for in that case both blood flows would have been smeared and would have overlapped each other. *"After extensive experimentation, this theory was recently shown to be untenable."*[31] The width and irregularity of flow 2 allows us to sense the pain and suf-

---

31 Frederick T. Zugibe, *The man of the shroud was washed*, http://e-forensicmedicine.net/Washed.htm

fering that such movements caused.

The formation of the straight flow 1 definitely requires some blood pressure. The crucified man must in any case have still been alive as he hung motionless on the cross. Had he been dead, this blood flow would not have been produced, for it is impossible that a corpse in this position, with arms outstretched and hands positioned above the heart, could have bled so.

Could it be that these blood flows first formed after the removal of the body from the cross as is sometimes claimed?[32] The answer is that flow 2 is as expected if the body was still hanging on the cross. Such a wound **had to bleed**, and the blood had to run down in exactly that direction on the arm. It is also to be expected that the body, upon loss of consciousness, shifted to one side, whereby the position of the arms and thus the course of the blood would automatically change. One blood flow, due to the movements of the live body on the cross, is wider and more irregular, the other flow narrow and straight. When a body is lying horizontally, only bleeding as in blood flow 3 can be expected; and only if the body is still alive.

The blood flows on the right hand, therefore, allow only one conclusion: The man on the Shroud must have hung only unconsciously until his body was removed from the cross. Otherwise, bloodstain 1 could not have formed.

Also found on the Shroud is blood that flowed from many smaller wounds on the back of the head. It comes from wounds that were caused by the crown of thorns. When this crown was removed during the removal of the body from the cross, the wounds, which until then had been plugged by the thorns, opened. In the case of a corpse, no more blood would have flowed here because the exterior blood vessels contract upon death. Corpses, therefore, look empty of blood or "pale as a corpse." Yet the many distinct bloodstains on the back of the head here are clearly recognizable as blood that could only have flowed in the grave. Should the blood have come out of the (living) body on the cross, it would have dried out and not soaked the shroud in the tomb as it did.

Could the body perhaps have been washed during burial, whereby blood can flow from wounds on a corpse? As the blood flows on the arms show, the body was obviously not washed. Had the hair been wetted, the blood would have mixed with the water and spread itself around equally in the hair. There is no way that such clearly delimited bloody spots, as are observable on the Turin Shroud, could have come from a corpse.

---

32 Ibid.

Rigor Mortis

According to overwhelming scientific opinion, rigor mortis begins about thirty minutes after death, forms completely within three to six hours, and then dissipates after thirty-six to ninety hours. In a case where a person has suffered greatly shortly before death, rigor mortis can set in completely within an hour of death. Medical examiners who have studied the Turin Shroud are—to the extent that they assume the Shroud covered a dead body—unanimous in the opinion that, at the time of the removal of the body from the cross, rigor mortis must have been complete.

Rigor mortis is seen in the stiffness of the extremities, the retraction of the thumbs and the distension of the feet. It has frozen an attitude of death while hanging by the arms; the rib cage is abnormally expanded, the large pectoral muscles are in an attitude of extreme inspiration.[33]

Yet Professor Bonte came to the following contrary result: *"I want to clearly deny, whether one can read the beginnings of rigor mortis in any of the diagnostic findings on the burial shroud. The position as it can be seen on the Shroud can in my opinion also be taken by a living person, that is, a seemingly dead man."*[34]

After the man of the Shroud hanging on the cross lost consciousness, his body slumped from an upright position with his arms widespread, his knees bent, and his head leaning forward and down due to gravity. The body must have completely stiffened in this position. One would have had to break the position of the arms with considerable force and bind them together with a wrist band, though no trace of this effort is visible in the image.

Julia Felzmann[35]

---

33 William Meacham, *The Rape of the Shroud*, 2005, p. 4.

34 Herbst, p. 100.

35 Inspired by: "*The Way of the Cross in the light of the Holy Shroud*" by Msgr. Giulio Ricci.

Since the degree of illumination in the image derives directly from the distance of the Shroud to the body at each separate location (the less distance, the more "image substance" on that spot and the darker the area in question), this distance can be fairly well calculated from the respective degree of illumination.[36] The following images show the position of the upper part of the body together with the Shroud (dashed line).

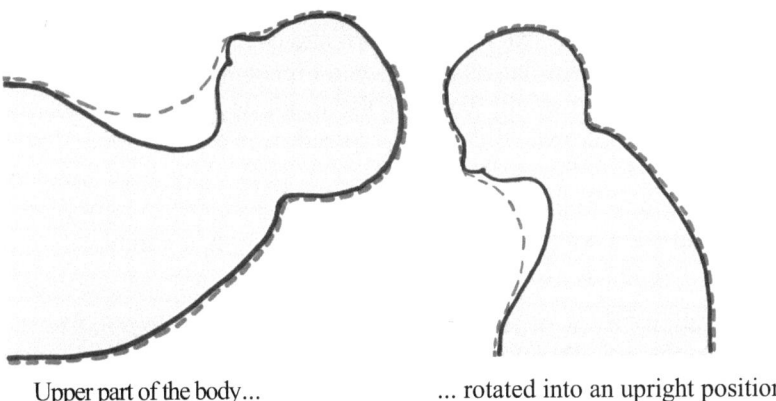

Upper part of the body...   ... rotated into an upright position

If one assumes that the body was laid in its grave in a stiffened position, the following questions or problems appear:

The arms were spread apart. The position of the arms in the grave, however, could have been forced by means of breaking their rigor mortis, but nothing indicates this. The arms seem to lie quite relaxed on the front of the body.

The position of the head raises larger questions. At the time of death, or of loss of consciousness, the head must have fallen forward and down due to gravity, whereby the chin must have almost touched the chest. The position of the head in the illustration "upper part of the body" reflects the position of the head in the tomb. This posture is very different from this posture on the cross. Muscular strength would have been necessary to hold the head in the position indicated by the shroud. This becomes immediately clear by turning the illustration around ninety degrees. The position of the head thus cannot be harmonized with rigor mortis. It may be that here, too, the rigor was

36 See degree thesis by C. Mungai, tutor Prof. G. Fanti: *Correlation Analysis between Luminance and Distance of Images Having 3-D Characteristics* at http://www.dim.unipd.it/misure/fanti/Mungai.ppt

forcibly broken, but the question remains as to why.

At the back of the head and the nape of the neck, the Shroud had direct contact with the body, and the image even follows the curve of the nape. The Shroud was clearly not tied with bands around the neck. Otherwise, the image would have been distorted. Therefore, the head and back must have lain on a kind of pillow. This can be deduced from the curious fact that the image of the back side of the man is actually longer than that of his front side. The body must, therefore, have lain slightly bent or hunched. Also, the hands would not reach so far down and cover the genitalia on the image if the body had lain flat, as anyone can immediately test on himself. Furthermore, the image of the back of the head, as well as that of the bloodstains from the crown of thorns, is spread over a larger area. These point to a soft support of some kind on which the back of the head was supported. If the head were instead elevated into free space due to rigor mortis and the Shroud were wrapped around it in that position, a completely different picture would have resulted in this area.

In the illustration "Back of the body" the wounds of the flogging to the calves and thighs are clearly visible. Thus, the distance between the legs and the Shroud could only have been very narrow. Due to gravity, the Shroud must have lain flat on the surface under it as indicated in the painting of Battista below. Otherwise, the Shroud—as in the case of a mummy—would have to have been wrapped tightly around the body or tied up. This scenario is excluded because images and bloodstains would then have been visible on the side areas of the body, and the image itself would have been distorted, which is not the case. Everything, therefore, points to the assumption that both the Shroud and the legs laid flat on the ground. This, too, is not in agreement with the body position on the cross; the feet could not have become stiff in such a straight position.

If all the features of the Shroud are looked at carefully, it is obvious that it did not wrap a body in rigor. On the other hand, everything fits exactly if we assume a living body. Here it may be remarked that, in the case of the wounds of scourging, it is not blood that we see (except for tiny isolated traces). Rather, these wounds are a part of the body image, a subject we will examine later.

Here is another important point: Nowhere on the Shroud has any sign of the onset of bodily decay been discovered.

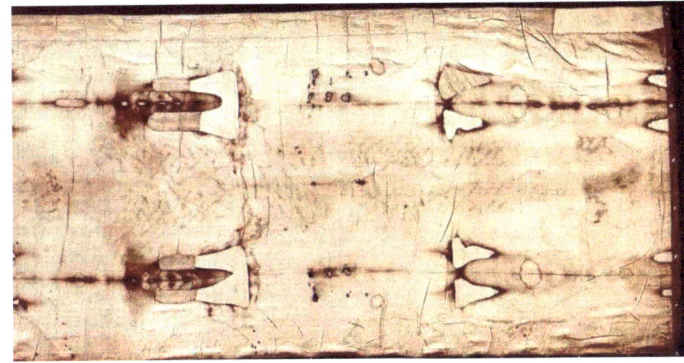

(15) Back of the body (Enrie)

(16) This sixteenth-century painting by Giovanni Battista shows how the body could have been wrapped in a burial shroud in a position that would match the image on the Shroud of Turin.

The Spanish pathologist Dr. Miguel Lorente published a book in which he explains that from the evidence of vitality and the absence of signs of death on the cloth, it has to be concluded that the man under the Shroud must have still been alive.[37]

For instance he argues that the invisible thumbs are a sign for life:

"...it was argued that the thumbs did not appear in the image on the Shroud due to cadaveric stiffness, which would cause the thumb to retract beneath the palm. Recent studies by Zugibe, however, have proven that even if there is an injury to the median nerve, cadaveric stiffness does not provoke a muscular contraction that moves the thumb beneath the hand. Instead, it remains in its usual position, next to the index finger.

When these studies are applied to the Shroud, where the thumbs are hidden beneath the palms, they indicate that the thumb placement is not a postmortem phenomenon, but rather that it can be provoked by a muscular hypertony due to hypocalcaemia produced by traumatic shock. It would therefore be a sign of vitality, as we have previously explained.."[38]

---

37 Miguel Lorente, *42 Diaz - Análisis forense de la crucifixión y la resurrección de Jesucristo*, El País Aguilar, 2007.

38 Miguel Lorente Acosta,Forensic Doctor, University of Granada, Forensic Analysis of the Image and Bloodstains on the Shroud of Turin: Contributions to the Evaluation of the Circumstances Surrounding the Death of Jesus of Nazareth, Based on the book: "42 days. Forensic analysis on the crucifixion and resurrection of Jesus of Nazareth, www.shroud.info/Lorente.pdf

The Formation of the Image

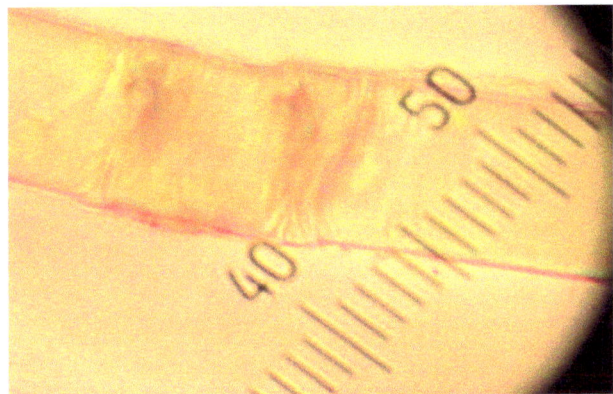

Microscopic photograph of an image-fibre. The image-substance is a thin, yellow coating on parts of the fibre. Courtesy R. Rogers

The image on the Shroud is not a contact print, for the image bears details of places on the body that must have been up to two inches away from the Shroud. Pure diffusion processes alone are thus eliminated because an image of such photographic clarity could never have formed that way.

There is, therefore, a broad consensus among Shroud researchers that the formation of the image must have something to do with energy. If a dead and thus relatively cold body is assumed, there is no known process that would explain the formation of such an image. How can the appearance of an appropriate form of energy in this scenario be explained? Many Christian believers, therefore, assume a kind of energy flash—perhaps resulting from high voltage—which was generated at the resurrection and which somehow branded or singed the image of the body onto the Shroud. But Rogers has found that *"any photon or particle with an energy above about 3 eV (e.g., light with a shorter wavelength than green)"* cause traces (defects) on the fibers, which can be seen under a microscope. As image fibers do not have more defects than nonimage fibers, he concluded that *"the image could not have involved energetic radiation of any kind; photons, electrons, protons, alpha particles, and/or neutrons."*[39]

In the area of blood stains, there is no image. Blood in image-areas has no other characteristics than blood outside these areas. If the image has been formed by direct exposure to energy (Corona Discharge, high-energy laser beams, "Energy Flash" during the resurrection), then the substance

---

39 Raymond N. Rogers, *The shroud of Turin: radiation effects, aging and image formation* at   http://www.shroud.com/pdfs/rogers8.pdf

of which the image consists today were originally part of the linen fibers, which have been altered (damaged) through the exposure of energy. This exposure of energy should have altered also the blood-substance. However, this is simply not the case. Rogers suggested therefore, that the image must have been formed under "mild conditions".

Thus in summary, it can be stated: the evidence points clearly against any form of intensive, high-energy radiation having caused the formation of the image. In addition, of course, there is the problem to explain scientifically, how such a high-energy radiation could have come out of a human body so suddenly.

If a solution is to be found based on scientific reasoning, **everything** research found out about the properties of the image has to be looked at very closely? Precise examination of linen fibers that are found in the area of the image has yielded the following information:[40]

- The yellowish chemical substance made up of doubly bound saccharides is present only on the **surface** of the fibers, which seen from a certain distance gives the impression of a body image. The fibers themselves are unchanged. Inside the fibers, neither discoloration nor any other change can be discovered.

- Not all threads in the image area are affected by this yellowish substance. Lying directly next to the threads affected by the image substance are also threads whose surfaces are unchanged and having no image-creating substance.

- The formation of the image must have occurred at a relatively low temperature (air or body temperature). The image cannot have been formed by heat scorching, because in that case the colors reflected under ultraviolet radiation would have a different spectrum than that found during the examination process. The image areas differentiate themselves here significantly from the areas that were scorched in the sixteenth-century fire at Chambery. We can therefore also assume that the process of image formation required a certain amount of time.

- The yellowish substance is found all around the affected fibers/fibrils, including areas on the sides opposite to the body. If the image had resulted from a direct energy effect, the energy would have had

---

40 Raymond N. Rogers und Anna Arnoldi, *Scientific method applied to the Shroud of Turin—A Review*, at http://www.shroud.com/pdfs/rogers2.pdf

to been so strong that it would have discolored the interior of the fibers before it had caused a discoloration of the opposite side of the fibers, which is not the case.

* In the case of the top half of the Shroud, that is, the half that lay over the front of the body, a very faint image is also recognizable on some areas of the opposite side, especially in the face area. The body image was thus formed on both sides of the cloth in some places.[41]

At the beginning of the twentieth century, Paul Vignon in his book *The Shroud of Christ* argued that the image formation process must have resulted from gases.[42] Vignon assumed that the applied substances of myrrh, aloes, and olive oil, as sensitizing agents, dampened the linen material. Experiments showed that chemical changes formed in connection with the gas ammonia, led to a gradual yellowing of a test cloth. Ammonia or amines form not only during the decay of corpses but also during the decay of urea. Parents know the strong smell of urea that arises from the changing of diapers. Admittedly, urea normally does not occur on the skin. Vignon discovered, however, that urea occurs abundantly in death perspiration, as well as in perspiration produced by a person being brutally tortured.[43]

The American chemist Raymond Rogers, who spent long years investigating the Shroud, examined in detail the chemical mechanisms that might have been responsible for the formation of the image on it. He was thereby able to offer an explanation for why some fibers contain the image-making substance, while some do not, even when they lie directly adjacent. During the linen production in antiquity, the spun linen fibers were individually moistened with a paste made of crude starch so that the threads could be more easily woven. Some fibers were moistened more than others. The finished Shroud was washed in a solution of saponaria officinalis, a soap-like plant solution, and then laid out to dry. On the surface of the fibers, there remained a thin, irregular coating of residual starch, which then reacted with the gases that arose from the body, forming the yellowish substance that produced the image. This explains why the yellowish substance is found only on the surface of the fibers, and also why there are neighboring fibers that do not contain this substance.

41 Giulio Fanti and Roberto Maggiolo, *The double superficiality of the frontal image of the Turin shroud*, Journal of Optics A: Pure and Applied Optics, 6, 2004.

42 Paul Vignon, *Le linceul du Christ*, Paris, 1902.

43 Rodney Hoare, *The Turin Shroud is Genuine*, 1998, p. 56 ff.

Rogers could experimentally reproduce this cause-and-effect process. Also, the fact that the image was formed in some places of the exterior of the Shroud can thus be explained. A portion of the gas diffused itself through the Shroud and reacted with the coating on the surface of the fibers on the other side.

The hypothesis that gases caused the formation of the image seems irrefutable, as only so is the effect through distance explicable. It is clear that the image can not be a pure contact-image, because parts of the body are visible, which must have had a distance of up to 2 inches to the surface of the body.

Rogers assumed that the image was formed by means of a complicated chemical process. He believed also that the man under the Shroud was dead, but the body still had certain residual warmth. The coating on the image-fibers was caused, according to this hypothesis, mainly by amines, which exited the skin due to initial decomposition processes. They reacted with the starch on the linen fibers and thus formed the yellowish coating. Rogers explained that the image substance is allocated on the Shroud in a way that gives the impression of a photograph because of a differentiated concentration of gases and possibly also differences of temperature, among other things. In our e-mail exchanges he admitted that the brilliance of the image cannot be explained by his hypothesis and that therefore this problem is not yet completely solved.

There are indeed a whole series of problems in this approach. The volume of the gas between the body and the Shroud was relatively small. New ammoniac (or amines as a product of decomposition, if one assumes a corpse) was permanently formed on the skin, which exited into the surrounding air and then either diffused through the Shroud or was used up during the formation of the image. It is, therefore, to be expected that equilibrium was established underneath the Shroud, where the amine gas concentration should have been rather steady in the volume between body and cloth, regardless of the distance from Shroud to skin.

A corpse would certainly have had residual warmth in the grave. This warmth would have led to air movement. This in turn would have led to a mixing of the gases and the hindering of the formation of different gas concentrations in the precisely required amounts. An even yellowing of the Shroud would be expected, like a big yellow stain, but not a high-resolution, photograph-like image. Objects are clearly recognizable, such as the upper lip, which must have been up to five centimeters (two inches) from the Shroud.

In the Near East but also in other parts of the world, people have been, and are, buried in shrouds or in cloth sacks. They are laid to rest not only in the raw earth but in grave chambers and catacombs. If it were so simple for a corpse and a shroud sprinkled with starch to yield an image, many such images on grave shrouds would have already been produced. Furthermore, it would be very simple today to reproduce a shroud with such an image. One would simply lay a shroud with such a preparation on the face of a corpse and wait for two days. Yet the image on the Turin Shroud is unique. A second such image of a corpse on a shroud has not been found, nor has it been possible to reproduce such an image experimentally.

This does not necessarily mean that the image was formed by supernatural forces. Nevertheless, a unique constellation of events must have arisen in the grave and led to a unique process.

Every body that is warmer than its surrounding temperature radiates energy in the form of infrared radiation. Poor conductors like the human body radiate this energy primarily in a vertical direction.[44] The energy radiation of a body decreases with distance. Rodney Hoare carried out the following experiment. A cloth was laid for some time on a man wearing only a swimming suit. Afterward, the cloth was held up and photographed with a temperature-sensitive camera. The photograph clearly showed a picture of heat on the shroud that the body had projected earlier. The less distance between body and shroud, the higher the temperature of the shroud on that spot.

The speed of the chemical process that produced the image substance (Maillard reaction) depends largely on the temperature. Between air temperature and body temperature, a rise of ten degrees Celsius can mean a doubling or even a tripling of the speed of the process.[45]

The chemical reaction can, therefore, cause a "heat picture" to materialize. The higher the temperature was on a certain spot on the shroud, the more image-producing substance formed, an effect directly related to the distance of the shroud to the body. As already shown, this effect leads to the impression of a photograph-like image, from which even a 3-D image can be produced.

If one assumes a corpse, it must be accepted that this body had certain residual warmth, which according to the described effect mechanism could also cause an image. Nevertheless,

44 Rogers, p. 11.
45 Ibid., p. 12.

the depth of staining over the length of the front and back of the body [image on the shroud] is fairly constant, so the temperature of the cloth must also have been approximately uniform. This could only happen if the blood were still circulating, the heart just beating. The body must have been in a coma, therefore, and not clinically dead by twentieth-century standards.

As soon as a body dies, its heart stops beating, and the blood is no longer forced round the body keeping the temperature nearly even. Very soon the extremities—feet, hands, nose—which have a large surface area compared with the matter they hold, cool down to the outside temperature. The trunk of the body and the head hold a very great deal of heat and will retain this for many hours. Not only that, but the blood no longer kept circulating, will naturally fall through gravity, causing lividity on the bottom surface. Some of these places, the buttocks and shoulder blades in a prone body, for instance, would therefore stay warm even longer, so that the signs of that warmth should have been visible as darker areas on the Shroud. Had it covered a dead body, the forensic experts would have expected no stain at all towards the feet, and the hands and nose would also have shown much less stain than they do.[46]

In connection with the image, there are three further observations that point to a living organism under the Shroud:

- The nose and the region under the nose belong to the darkest areas of the image. In the case of a corpse, the opposite would be expected, since the nose area cools down more quickly than other parts of the body. Warm air from the lungs would result in stronger discoloration.

- The image in the area of the head is darker than elsewhere. In the case of a corpse, there is no explanation for such a thing. A living organism, however, under heavy loss of blood, directs more blood into the brain and inner organs, which results in relative temperature differences, and thus differences of lightness in the image.

- The wounds of the flogging are a part of the body image and are not bloodstains. This, too, is easily explicable. Skin wounds lead to a light rising of the skin temperature in the area of the wounds (about one or two degrees Celsius). As with the rest of the image, a higher temperature causes the formation of more image sub-

---

46 Hoare, p. 69. Result of the examination of the image by forensic scientists.

stance, and thus the areas in question appear darker, which precisely matches the observations.

However, nobody has yet succeeded in producing a comparable image experimentally. The reason is that a test person would have to be treated the same way as the man under the Shroud. He would also have to lay under a cloth motionless for a while. We also do not know which substances (ointments, oils, spices, and so on) were used during the burial or during the production of the cloth. Therefore, we do not know the exact chemical situation under the shroud. An important step for an experimental verification is, therefore, to analyze the image formation process in several parts.

One question is, for instance, whether a warm body can project a temperature image onto a cloth laid upon it. In order to test this, I laid a piece of cloth over a rubber glove filled with warm water for a short time, then put the cloth aside, and photographed it immediately with a temperature-sensitive camera.

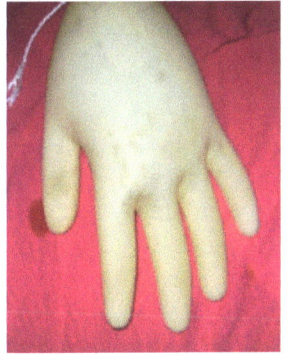  

Warm rubber glove   Thermo image ©H. Felzmann   converted into 3D[47]

An infrared camera converses temperatures in colors or brightness (the warmer, the brighter). A warm body indeed projects a temperature image on a cloth laid upon it. That a chemical process follows this temperature distribution and thus materializes a temperature image can be assumed. The characteristic of the allocation of the image substance on the Shroud corresponds with the characteristics of the temperature allocation on a cloth laid on a warm body. As the image substance darkens the surface of the Shroud, a point on the image becomes darker when the temperature is higher, which happens in places where the distance to the body is shorter.

47 Computed by Dr. Gerardo Ballabio

Therefore, the thermo image has to be compared with the negative of the Shroud image. It is possible to convert the thermo image into a 3D-image by using a VP8- image converter software. The congruence with the optical characteristics of the image on the shroud is remarkable.

In 1981 in a Liverpool hospital, a mattress was found that bore the image of one hand and the buttocks of a just-deceased cancer patient. This image had similarities to the image on the Shroud of Turin.[48] Thus, under certain chemical circumstances, it is entirely possible that a warm, living body can cause an image to form.

That the Turin Shroud bears a photograph-like image, as well as its fresh blood and the lack of rigor mortis on the man in the image is further indication that the man under the Shroud must have been alive.

Granted, almost all Shroud researchers assume the Shroud contained a dead body.[49] In general, most of these researchers are traditional Christians who strictly reject any argument that could suggest that Jesus survived the cross. Such a thought is even considered a kind of heresy. Much is at stake here. From their perspective, it must be a tragedy that the object that appears to lend credibility to their faith should instead become proof that the central belief of their faith might have no historical basis.

True scientific research has always to be without fixed expectations regarding the results. Unfortunately, what is often lacking here is the required scientific neutrality. At present, these matters seem utterly polemical. Dr. Frederick Zugibe, an American medical examiner, writes in his book: *In general, the Swoon Theory is completely unfounded and is refuted by the following facts: First, Jesus' physical condition was grave. The extent and severity of His injuries dictate that He would not have survived the crucifixion. Second, no medications or drugs of the time would have been able to stop the excruciating pains Jesus was undoubtedly experiencing, and no drugs of the time were capable of placing Him into a deep sleep to feign death given His condition. . . . Those authors who used the Shroud as evidence that Jesus was alive after removal from the cross were either ignorant of or disregarded medical and scientific evidence to the contrary. Moreover, the presence of rigor mortis, noted on the Shroud and acknowledged by well-known forensic and general*

---

48 Google:" Jospice mattress", result, e.g., http://www.shroud.com/pdfs/mattress.pdf

49 This refers also to the members of the shroud science group.

pathologists, attests to this.[50]

The conviction that the man on the Shroud must have been dead is sustained by two major arguments:

1. Jesus, so badly wounded after the crucifixion, could not have acted as is reported of him.

2. It is impossible to survive the type of injuries Jesus sustained.

The first case involves in an unacceptable confusion of religion and science. On this point, it must be a question exclusively of the Shroud. In order to eliminate bias as much as possible, it is even required to leave the possibility that it could involve the historical Jesus. Thus, only the information taken from the Shroud may be evaluated because the information on the Shroud is far more objective than texts that were written decades after the events.

The second point reveals the poor relationship between what is seen and what would normally be accepted as certain. Of course, it is absolutely improbable to sustain such wounds and thereafter be entombed while still alive and survive the ordeal. On the other hand, if a person is still breathing and the pupils react to light, no one would come to the conclusion that the person is dead, no matter how serious the injuries might be. The direct evidence for life thus takes priority over general observations such as the severity of the wounds, pain suffered, and so on.

Nevertheless, it is repeatedly stated that at the latest, the thrust with the lance into the side of Jesus, as seen imaged on the Shroud, must have led to his death because it went directly into his heart. However, no exit wound is visible. The lance only entered the body partially, and therefore one can determine nothing about the direction and the deepness of the lance thrust. In other words, if the man was still alive thereafter, as a series of indications clearly show, the lance could not have hit the heart.

How dangerous was that side wound? The English researcher Rodney Hoare, while chairman of the British Society of the Turin Shroud, wrote in his book how he visited a team of medical examiners with enlarged photographs of the Shroud of Turin. His intention was to let such experts explain the cause of death. To the question of the severity of the lance thrust into the chest, he received the following surprising answer:

"That would have done little damage. Put your hand where the point en-

---

50 Frederick Zugibe, *The Crucifixion of Jesus—A Forensic Inquiry*, p. 161f.

tered as on the Shroud photograph, and then lift your arms to the side in the crucifixion position, and it was too high to damage anything if the wound came from below. It would have bled, as we can see, and it might have allowed water between the lung and its cavity to come out at the same time. That water, the pleural effusion, would have been formed when the body was scourged. The lung would have been forced back, but even if the weapon had entered the lungs they can localize the injury." Then I asked, if the chest wound could not have been fatal, what did the man die of?

For perhaps thirty minutes they discussed this before I had a consensus report. It was this: "If he lived before the seventeenth century, he would have been dead. He may have been unconscious on the cross and barely breathing, so he would have been dead to the onlookers. That's what they looked for. After Harvey they would have tested his pulse which would have been beating weakly. If he had lived in the twentieth century he would have been certified as in a coma."[51]

The lance thrust was not intended to kill the crucifixion victim here. His death should have followed from the crucifixion itself. It was assumed that Jesus was already dead. The heart area would have been the most appropriate place for a deadly lance thrust. The reason for this lance thrust was far more to find out if the victim still showed any reaction to additional pain. The wound in the side was certainly a serious wound, but it occurred on a place of the body that would not lead to fatal injury.

Of course, you must decide for yourself which conclusions you would like to draw from all the facts and interpretations presented here. This book, however, assumes the theory of the natural survival of the man under the Turin Shroud, for the research results show that it is sufficiently plausible. The whole story is in itself incredible, but everything speaks for a natural course of events. There is thus no gap in the explanation needing the assumption of a supernatural event. If, however, the assumption is that there was a corpse under the Shroud, a gap develops in the explanation of the image formation because no satisfactory natural explanation for the formation of the image based on this scenario has been found, even after one hundred years of Shroud research. This is also why many people prefer to believe the Shroud to be a forgery. The argument usually goes something like this:[52]

---

51 Hoare, p. 68.

52 See, for example, David Roemer's "Why the Turin Shroud Is Not Authentic" at http://www.dkroemer.com/shroud.html

- Science has more or less proven that a corpse cannot produce such an image.

- Miracles are only in the heads of people and do not occur in actual historical events.

- Therefore, there is strong evidence that the image on the Shroud must be man-made.

The problem for shroud skeptics is that the Shroud is simply too good to have been forged. As Einstein said, if a problem cannot be solved within a certain paradigm, it is necessary to change the paradigm and look for a solution then.

Was the Man under the Shroud Jesus?

Can we really know such a thing for sure? Is such a statement even acceptable in a strictly scientific sense? Of course not! No statement about the past can be proven one hundred percent because we cannot experimentally repeat the past.

Were human beings really on the moon forty years ago, and did they walk around on its surface? Was the whole thing perhaps a masterly Hollywood production, an ingenious fake that everyone has believed, a gigantic conspiracy with the goal of gaining special credit for the USA during the Cold War? Can we exclude that notion completely? One needs only to search on the Internet to find abundant "proofs" of a "conspiracy," proof that includes photographs and films.[53]

Nevertheless, it is claimed—and rightly, I believe—that the Apollo space mission landed on the moon, even though no one can be absolutely certain without being directly involved in the project. The French philosopher Rene Descartes remarked: "The only thing that we really know for certain is that we exist." Apparently, there remains for us nothing but to acknowledge everything as reality, even if we are not one hundred percent certain and cannot prove it.[54]

Can you, in this modest sense, believe that an actual crucified man once lay under the Shroud of Turin? If so, good. Then it is only a matter of asking whether that man was the authentic Jesus (the historical Jesus of Nazareth). We will never be able to know that with one hundred percent certainty, but perhaps the collective evidence is enough for us to believe. Let's, therefore, look into the matter more deeply. The evidence can be categorized in three ways: the first type, possible evidence; the second type, probable evidence; and the third type, certain evidence. A "false Jesus" would have to fit all three types.

There is, moreover, no evidence at all to say that the man of the Shroud image is someone other than Jesus—with one exception, the evidence of

---

53 Search terms like "moon landing fake" lead to sites like http://www.ufos-aliens.co.uk/cosmicapollo.html, "The faked Apollo landings."

54 In the movie *The Matrix*, this truth is carried to extremes. Humans, whose bodies have been connected to machines, experience internally a regular, modern life, which is fed in directly into their brains electronically, and everybody believes that this is the only reality.

the 1988 carbon 14 dating results, which dated the Shroud fabric to the Middle Ages, but that issue will be treated in detail in the next chapter.

If anything on the Shroud did not fit with our knowledge of the historical Jesus of Nazareth—for example, if the man depicted had broken legs—the matter would be settled instantly. He could not be Jesus. Any further discussion would be moot, even if everything else seemed to fit.

All four Gospels reported that the body of Jesus was wrapped in a shroud (or in grave cloths): "*Joseph of Arimathea bought a large sheet, took Jesus from the cross, wrapped him in the sheet and laid him in a grave*" (Mark 15:46). On Easter morning Peter and John found the shroud in the tomb "*folded together on the side*" (John 20:6–7).

Thus, there was indeed a shroud for Jesus. The question is, could this shroud really have been preserved over a period of 2000 years, and could it be identical to the Shroud of Turin?

Evidence of the First Type (Possible Evidence)[55]

Here the question is, above all, whether the Turin Shroud is authentic in the sense that a real, crucified man once lay under it, and whether it could derive from antiquity. This issue can be treated quickly because so much evidence of this kind has already been presented in earlier chapters.

Can fabrics even be preserved so long? Yes. In the tombs of the pharaohs, cloths have been found that are thousands of years older than the Shroud. There were also such types of cloths in Syria–Palestine at the time of Jesus.[56]

In the first third of the fourth century, the Emperor Constantine forbade the practice of crucifixion. Therefore, the Shroud with its image of a crucified man must have come from a period before that. Anyone who might conceivably have crucified a person later in order to forge a shroud "relic" would certainly have driven the nails through the palm of the hands, as all artists have represented this detail of the crucifixion of Jesus. Yet the image on the Shroud of Turin reveals that the nails were driven through the base, not palms, of the hands.

---

55 Compare the following text with Herbst, p. 79 and following.

56 The master textile restorer Mechthild Flury-Lemberg stated, "The linen cloth of the Shroud of Turin does not display any weaving or sewing techniques which would speak against its origin as a high-quality product of the textile workers of the first century." Section "Shroud of Turin" in www.cs.mcgill.ca/

51

Likewise, no medieval painter would have left the thumbs of the man un-visible, as the Shroud image does, because no such painter would have known that a penetration of the base of the hand would have injured the median nerve, which is so close to the thumb, and would thus have drawn the thumb inward toward the palm.

Could the image have been painted on the Shroud? No. Even when viewed in enlargements magnified a thousand times, the Shroud reveals no trace of paint, and no adhesion of the fibers can be seen.

Anyone who might have wanted to falsify the blood evidence could not have used animal blood for his scheme. The bloodstains on the Shroud are human blood, as the medical examiner and Shroud researcher Dr. Bollone has proven. Any such painter, moreover, would also have to have applied all such bloodstains to the Shroud before applying its body image because no traces of that body image appear under those bloodstains. The blood must have come first, the image second—how improbable for a painter to have done things so. Moreover, the image is a vague one, its lightness and darkness not based on the normal perception of the eye but dependent solely on the distance of the cloth from the body at each point. There is not a shadow of evidence that there has been a tradition of artists inventing techniques to create pieces of art with such characteristics. The shroud is absolutely unique.

Evidence of a Second Type (Probable Evidence)

Here the markers of a specific person, Jesus of Nazareth, increase consid-erably. Yet it could still be a matter of some other person's image on the cloth.

Crucified persons were left hanging on their crosses until their bodies were thrown into a grave. The crucified man of the Shroud, however, was honorably buried in an accessible tomb. Otherwise, the Shroud would never have been preserved.

The process of crucifixion aimed for the slowest possible death, which often took several days. In case of a need to remove the bodies sooner, the lower legs of the crucified were deliberately broken by soldiers at-tending the execution so that the crucified would have no support and, hanging limp and being unable to breathe in that position, would quickly suffocate. Yet in the case of the crucified man of the Shroud, the legs were not broken, as can clearly be seen. However, his chest was speared, precisely as in the case of Jesus reported in the Gospel of John. Jesus had been considered dead after only a few hours on the cross, and that spear thrust was made to ensure that he was dead.

The crucified man of the Shroud was also wrapped, unwashed, in the Shroud and was left in the tomb as if there were no time for an orderly burial, just as in the case of Jesus as reported in the Gospels. He could only be buried provisionally, so soon before the beginning of the Sabbath.

This crucified person was also buried by a very rich man who could afford a rock tomb, as well as a shroud, which at the time must have been very expensive. Such was the "wealthy councilor Joseph of Arimathea," a secret follower of Jesus.

The plants and blossoms that were laid on the body and which were also imaged on the Shroud can be matched precisely to the place and season of the burial of Jesus: Jerusalem in April. The coins on the eyes, if considered as evidence, can likewise be dated to about the year AD 30.

Evidence of a Third Type (Certain Evidence)

This type of evidence I would characterize as certain because it applies only to Jesus and no other possible person. The events surrounding the crucifixion of Jesus reveal a number of unique details, which taken together did not occur a second time in history. Whoever would claim the contrary should offer some counterevidence. Since these details are all mirrored in the Turin Shroud, a clear assignment is possible without any ifs or buts.

For example, the Romans crucified many Jews as enemies of the state in Palestine. Yet this one seen on the Shroud must have ranked as a very high leader because the Roman soldiers placed upon his head an oriental crown made of thorn twigs in order to humiliate him as an upstart king, just as Jesus was humiliated according to the Gospels.[57]

Again, it was impossible that anyone executed as a traitor could be honorably buried without the special permission of the Roman occupation

---

57 Evidence: the blood on the back head. Prof. Danin and Dr. Uri Baruch from the University of Jerusalem have identified many pollen and some images of Gundelia tournefortii on the shroud. It is a thistle with very sharp, thorn-like leaves, which they assume to have formed the crown of thorns.
See http://www.shroudstory.com/pollen.htm

power. But "Joseph of Arimathea took courage and went to Pilate" to ask such permission. And Pilate, though despised as brutal, gave his approval.

If the body so buried had remained untouched in its tomb, the Shroud would have decayed with it, but Jesus did not remain in his tomb.

That the shroud of Jesus was preserved proves that the friends of the crucified man did not believe him dead. For people of the Jewish tradition, anything that had touched a corpse was considered "impure" and would not be retained.

The man of the Shroud, though humiliated and crucified as "King of the Jews," was not honored as a martyr by average Jews but only by the new Christian Jews, who would preserve his shroud as a holy relic through the centuries.[58]

Not only was the Shroud preserved but its image was from the beginning considered as holy and "not made by hands" but by a supernatural power, God. Immediately it became the master for all images of Jesus. Therefore, all pictorial ideas about Jesus originated with the Shroud.

Is there a second person in all history who was crucified precisely as was Jesus, and was buried in an expensive sheet, and whose body did not decompose but somehow lived again, and who was still seen alive thereafter?

---

58 Evidence: Old history of the shroud. There is no tradition of a holy shroud with an image in Judaism, but there is one in the Eastern Orthodox Church.

The C14-dating fiasco

There will be hell to pay when the truth comes out.

Raymond N. Rogers, one of the most prominent
shroud scientists, about the C14-dating[59]

Seeing the Shroud of Turin is like seeing Jesus, standing before a skep-tical world that is interested only in facts, saying as he once said to Thomas: *"Put your finger here; see my hands. Reach out your hand and put it into my side. Stop doubting and believe"* (John 20:27). But there is one single research result that puts all these evidences into question.

In 1984, experts from the STURP team (scientists who had examined the cloth closely a few years earlier) proposed 26 scientific examinations to be carried out on the cloth, including radiocarbon dating. This proposal was approved by Cardinal Ratzinger.

Radiocarbon dating is based on the fact that a certain portion of the carbon in the air consists of radioactive carbon 14 isotopes. The isotopes decay with a regular half-life, but new isotopes are permanently formed in the highest layers of the atmosphere due to the sun's radiation, so that equilibrium is formed in the air. In a living organism, the ratio of these atoms exactly matches this ratio in the air. However, when the organism dies, the number of carbon 14 isotopes is reduced by half every 5730 years. Thus, the smaller the C14 ratio, the older the organic material must be.

A series of meetings were held over the next four years to plan the dat-ing. Participants were representatives from the Church, dating institutes, and the STURP team. A protocol was agreed upon which, however, was disregarded in almost all points during the subsequent implementation[60].

---

59 Quoted from the back cover of William Meacham's book, *The Rape of the Turin Shroud – How Christianity's most precious relic was wrongly condemned, and violated*, 2005

60 See the Youtube-Video „The Shroud of Turin 1988 Carbon Dating: Triumph or Travesty?" www.youtube.com/watch?v=JBDuKZSgDSI

Top	Agreed	Implementation
1	7 C14 laboratories involved	3 laboratories
2	2 dating methods	1 dating method
3	Direction: British Museum	
4	Test samples to be taken from 3 places on the cloth	Only from one place
5	STURP scientists select these spots and cut out samples	no
6	Laboratories date cloth samples together with 2 blank samples	Surprisingly, a third blind sample (threads)
7	Nobody should be able to recognize which sample was from the shroud	Everyone could recognize the blind samples immediately 1: 1 weave, shroud 3: 1 weave
8	Only authorized parties should see results beforehand	Agreement broken several times
9	Labs should test simultaneously - no information exchange	Arizona: Mai 88 Zurich: Juni 88 Oxford Juli 1988 Information was exchanged
10	3 other institutes carry out the statistical analysis	British Museum only!
11	At the end joint meeting of laboratories and statisticians to adopt the final result	no

The project participants should not be imagined as a harmonious group. There were different interests and prejudices. The laboratories were said to be primarily concerned with publicity and raising funds. The STURP members were seen as a bunch of religious zealots. Harry Gove, the spokesman for the laboratories, wanted to throw them out of the project entirely, because "almost without exception they are people who believe that the cloth is that of Christ. It is a fact that scientists who are firmly convinced of something can achieve practically any result." His efforts were successful insofar as the other 25 research proposals of the

STURP team were dropped and STURP was even excluded from point 5 of the protocol: selection of the sampling points, cutting out the samples. Since they had already worked on the shroud for five days, they were indeed predestined to pinpoint the best spots. Grove's lab also had to leave the project, because only 3 labs remained.

Raymond Rogers, a member of the STURP team, later stated that the worst possible spot had been chosen, a corner where the cloth was very often held in its history at exhibitions and was therefore heavily soiled. It was also near a burn mark.

One small piece from the Shroud of Turin was further divided into five pieces, four of them were sent to three renowned institutes; one larger piece was kept as a reserve. On October 13, 1988, Prof. E. Hall, Dr. M. Tite, and Dr. R. Hedges from the British Museum organized a press conference and announced the result: the Shroud dates with certainty from the thirteenth to the fourteenth centuries. Hall said later in an interview, *"We have shown the Shroud to be a fake. Anyone who disagrees with us ought to belong to the Flat Earth Society."* The Cardinal of Turin, Ballestrero, announced shortly thereafter that the Shroud had been proved to be a medieval forgery.

Only in the course of the next months and years did it become clear how this result had come about.

Taking the samples

The main players

Archbishop of Turin, Ballestrero: As the Catholic Church is the legal owner of the cloth, his role was that of a principal. He proclaimed already one day before the press conference in which the results were announced, that it is now proven that the cloth is a fake from the Middle Ages. In 1989 he went into **retirement** and was no longer available for questions.

Dr. Michael Tite: he was co-director of the British Museum, scientific coordinator of the project and placed by the cardinal as a guarantor of the honesty of the process. The Sunday Telegraph contained in its edition from 25th/26th March 1989 an article in which it was reported, *"that 45 businessmen and benefactors would give to the Oxford laboratory a donation of 1 million pounds, in order to establish a department of archae-*

ology and to secure the continuance of the laboratory, which has founded by Professor Edward Hall with his own financial resources. First Professor will be   Dr. Michael Tite from the British Museum."[61]

Giovanni Riggi (d. 2008): He was a member of the STURP-team and convinced of the authenticity of the cloth. His job was to cut out the samples. His conviction and his behavior suggest that he was not involved in an exchange.

Prof. Franco Testore (textile expert at the University of Turin): He received the cut out pieces from Riggi, carried each of them to the precision scale and gave it back to Riggi for the next cuttings.

Even the statements about the cutting out of the samples were contradictory. Giovanni Riggi, who cut out the samples and really should have known later what he had done, revised his oral and written statements several times.

During the shroud conference in Paris in 1989 Riggi stated that he first cut out a piece of 81 x 16 mm weighting 540 mg. On the video, made during the removal process, the scale, however, shows a weight of 478.1 mg. According to Testore the substance had a mass per unit area of 23 mg/cm^2. But 8.1 x 1.6 x 0.23, however, is 298 mg and not the displayed 478.1 mg. In a second step some edges were cut from this raw part. According to Riggi's first statement a piece of 7x1 cm remained with a weight of 300 mg. At least that is the information in the article in the journal Nature[62], in which the events and the result were finally published. But 7 x 1 x 0.23 results in only 161 mg.

The remaining piece was then divided into two parts, each of about 150 mg, "*one of them was then divided in 3 parts. Accidentally each of the resulting pieces was identical to the others. On an electronic scale the weight of these three pieces differed only by about 1 milligram from each other and their weights were nearly 53 mg*" (first statement of Riggi at the Paris conference) [63]

During this symposium he handed out a sketch, on which each of his cuts can be seen[64]

---

61 Wilson, p. 424.

62 www.shroud.com/nature.htm: Radiocarbon Dating of the Shroud of Turin

63 Kuhnke, p. 119

64 To bee seen in www.shroud.com/pdfs/n24part3.pdf

Prof. Testore writes in the first version of his official report for the symposium (page 3): "*The piece was divided into two more or less equal parts, with weights 154.9 mg for the first part and 144.8 mg for the second and a weighting loss of about 0.3 mg ... The first half was divided into three parts, which were almost identical: one weighed 52.0 mg, 52.8 mg the second and the third 53.7* mg".[65]

However the laboratory in Arizona received two pieces, therefore a total of four pieces must have been cut out! This fact was initially concealed, even in the Nature article nothing can be read about 4 pieces.

However, since this fact could no longer be hidden, Riggi and Testore corrected their statements. Testore later: "*The second piece, the smaller one, was divided into three parts: the first weighed 52.0 mg, the second 52.8 mg and the third 39.6 mg. In order to get the minimum weight for the third sample, from the first piece, a narrow strip of 14.1 mg was cut; therefore one of the three laboratories received two small rectangles from the shroud whose total weight was 53.7 mg* ".[66]

Riggi presented two further sketches, in the first sketch he followed Testore's revised version, which he again corrected later: the three major pieces had now been cut from the right, whilst the smaller main piece, (the small Arizona sample) was cut from the larger main piece.

What more can be said? If the key players do not remember what they exactly did, how trustworthy is the whole process? It is superfluous to mention that in the video, only the cutting out of three pieces is recorded .

During the cutting of the samples many witnesses were present and the entire procedure was videotaped. But then two men were alone with all this material in an adjoining room. In the Nature article we read: "*The samples were then taken to the adjacent Sala Capitolare where they were wrapped in aluminum foil and subsequently sealed inside numbered stainless-steel containers by the Archbishop of Turin and Dr. Tite.*" This is incredible! A notary would have been appropriate for this task, especially as it was done in secret. Ballestrero and Tite as the main actors of the project should have been the last choice for this task. This is clearly not correct scientific procedure! It is also not astonishing that there was no official protocol signed by any of the persons present. Even the cameraman who was supposed to record the entire process had to stay outside.

65 Herbst ,p. 142
66 Kuhnke, p. 123

This procedure interrupted the chain of evidence. Therefore the results of the dating are scientifically worthless. A chain is as strong as its weakest link. It therefore means nothing at all if the samples were originally cut out in front of many witnesses and cameras, but the packaging was then done in secret. Ethical science requires that results obtained under such dubious circumstances may not be used unless it is 100% proven that the samples that arrived at the institutes are identical to those that were cut from the shroud (reverse of the burden of proof).

One could overlook this fact if there weren't so many inconsistencies in this project. There are inexplicable differences in weight: The Zurich sample, at 52.8 mg, matched a piece measured in Turin. The two Arizona samples were weighed at 53.7 mg in Turin, but only 52.8 mg arrived in Arizona; the label on the packaging cylinder red 53.8 mg[67]. The Oxford sample weighed 50.0 mg, in Turin the remaining piece weighed 52,0 mg. The stay in the Sala Capitolare, away from witnesses and cameras, was much longer than it would have been necessary to pack samples.

The blind samples

They provided the official reason why the packing of the samples should be done in secret. Each institute received 4 samples at the end:

Sample 1: alleged piece of the shroud;
Sample 2: piece of linen from the 11th or 12th century;
Sample 3: Piece of linen from a grave in Thebes from the 2nd century;
Sample 4: threads from the choir mantle of St. Ludwig (1296/97).

The so-called shroud sample looks as if it has just come from the weaving mill. On the other hand, Ms. Flury-Lemberg, a textile expert who knows the cloth better than anyone else, writes that "*the Turin shroud is burdened with the dust of centuries and with greasy dirt deposits on the corners, a result of the countless handlings in the past - its weaving structure is cohesive and untouched even at the corners* [where samples were taken]"[68].

67 shroudstory.com/2013/05/05/the-arizona-samples-of-the-shroud-of-turin/
68 www.shroud.com/pdfs/n65part5.pdf

Sample 1: "Shroud"   Sample 2: 11./12. Century

Sampe 3: 2. Century

Unused Arizona samples   courtesy © STEA

Anyone can identify the blank samples immediately. Contrary to the originally agreed protocol, the institutes were informed in advance of the type and age of the control samples by Tite and Ballestrero[69]. The blanks were absolutely superfluous. The secret action in the back room was groundless, unless its purpose was to be able to exchange the samples comfortably and without witnesses. All blind samples were dated quite precisely, which speaks for the reliability of the C14 method and the institutes and against a measurement error of 1300 years in the shroud sample.

---

69 The letter is reprinted in Wilson, Das Turiner Grabtuch, p. 260

Statistical evaluation of the results[70]

Carbon dating is complex. One cannot expect that the exact same result will come out with every measurement. Therefore, several tests are carried out. A mean value and a standard deviation of the test results are obtained. The results of the blind samples were homogeneous in all three institutes, but not so with the shroud samples: There is almost no overlap between the age distributions of the Oxford and the Arizona samples, as if the samples came from different substances.

An indicator of how well the results agree is the "significance level": the higher the value, the more reliable the test. The values of the blank samples are between 30% and 90%. A value of only 5% was officially given for the shroud samples. If the value is below 5%, the results are definitely considered to be unreliable and the test should be rejected.

However, when one recalculated the published data, a value of 4.176% came out. A remarkable decision must have been made when the results were published anyway and the value rounded up contrary to the rule. The dating was then sold as irrefutable scientific truth. Perhaps someone has succumbed to the temptation of money and fame?

It takes revenge that, in disregard of the agreed protocol, the statistical evaluations were also carried out by the British Museum. That would be like abolishing the separation of powers in a democracy. But it got worse. Arizona ran not just four tests, as officially reported, but eight. The results were consolidated to four, averages were used without publishing this. If you take the eight values, the deviation from the results of the other two laboratories becomes even greater. The "significance level" was only 1.3%. When this became known[71], scientists requested the release of all raw data. The British Museum refused to do so. Finally, the surrender was forced by a court. It turned out that far more tests were conducted than published. The statistical unreliability of the test results was confirmed again.

Nevertheless, when the results were published in the journal Nature in 1988, a total of 21 scientists signed that the cloth came from the Middle Ages and that the results were reliable. It is therefore easily possible that the carbon dating of the Turin Shroud will go down in the history of science as one of its greatest fiascos.

---

70 The Shroud of Turin 1988 Carbon Dating: Triumph or Travesty?
youtube.com/watch?v=JBDuKZSgDSI
71 https://www.shroud.com/vanhels3.htm

In a way, the project was very successful. The result was a sensation and immediately spread all over the world. Today most people accept these results and consider the Turin cloth to be a fake from the Middle Ages, without knowing what feet of clay they are on.

It also paid off financially for Oxford: In the issue of March 25-26, 1989, an article appeared in the Sunday Telegraph according to which 45 businessmen and "wealthy patrons" made a donation of 1 million pounds to the Oxford Laboratory in order to ensure the continued existence of the laboratory that Professor Edward Hall had set up from his own resources. When he retired in 1989, his successor was Dr. Michael Tite. He was the project manager[72].

But we are not finished yet. Even if the test had to be repeated due to inaccuracies, this would hardly have changed the result (Middle Ages). However, if the cloth actually comes from ancient times, how did this result come about? There are three main attempts to explain this:

Thesis 1: Measurement error due to contamination

This thesis can be refuted easily. The contamination should be organic in nature: fungi, bacteria. Unorganic dirt does not contain carbon. Let us assume that this material came from the year 1800 on average. After that, the cloth was certainly so well taken care of that hardly any dirt should have been added. The proportion of organic contaminated material would have to be more than two and a half times the original cloth in order to move the result of a C14 analysis from the year 30 to the year 1300. This is completely impossible.

Thesis 2: The cloth was repaired in the Middle Ages

Cutting out the sample in only one place and in a corner where the cloth was very often held at ceremonies and exhibitions was certainly a crucial mistake. The thesis assumes that just in that area a piece of fabric has been so artfully replaced that nobody has noticed that indeed a medieval replacement has been cut out for the C14 test ("invisible mending theory"). During the Middle Ages the "invisible" repair of valuable cloths was indeed a highly developed art.

Dr. Mechthild Flury-Lemberg is an internationally renowned Swiss textile conservator. During the shroud-restoration carried out in 2002 she performed most of the work and has spent many hours in direct work on the cloth. She contradicted Rogers shortly after the publication of his arti-

---

72 Wilson, Das Turiner Grabtuch, 1999, S. 424.

cle - her statement in short: "In the sampling-area, there are no patches, otherwise we would have noticed them!" During the Dallas shroud-conference in 2005 she made a presentation, in which she refuted the "invisible mending theory".[73]

Her basic statements: A hole, elaborately darned, may be invisible on the front to the layman, but the expert will recognize it immediately - even with the naked eye. *"...In any case, neither on the front nor on the back of the whole cloth is the slightest hint of a mending operation, a patch or some kind of reinforcing darning, to be found."*[74]

Still: Nobody was there, maybe she was wrong and the repair was so perfect that even she didn't notice it? One thing is certain: there is no direct evidence that this thesis is correct.

Thesis 3: The samples were not from the shroud

Such a degree of foulness can be ruled out, therefore: fraud, a huge accusation! After all, there were many high-ranking people present when the sample was taken: a cardinal, professors, doctors - are they all supposed to have been part of a plot? The article with the results appeared in the renowned journal "Nature" and thus received highest scientific honors.

Of course, not everyone involved has to have participated in the plot, two or three people would have been enough, the rest (including the public) would have been fooled. There were allegations in this direction from the start. The professor and Jesuit Bulst, at that time the "Shroud Pope" in Germany, was one of the first to speak of fraud just a year after dating (1989)[75]. After that, other books were published in which various authors researched a fraud, sometimes independently of one another, and documented it in great detail. As far as I know, none of the attacked persons (the cardinal and Dr. Tite) legally defended themselves, so that no official investigations took place. There have been many details uncovered. Only the most serious indications of an exchange are presented here.

What made Prof. Bulst particularly suspicious was the statement made by Dr. Wölfli (laboratory in Zurich) about how clean and unpolluted the item received would have been. He knew the shroud very well. At the

---

73 http://www.shroud.com/pdfs/n65part5.pdf

74 www.shroud.com/pdfs/n65part5.pdf

75 Bulst 1990, Betrug am Grabtuch

area where the pieces were cut out, it was - as already shown - particularly dirty.

The most suitable time for an exchange was the secret packing of the samples in the next room. But how could the replacement piece (simili) have been obtained? Here, too, the pretext of procuring blind samples could have been an advantage, because this way a simili could have been searched openly.

The shroud was first exhibited in France in 1357, and since this period, the history of the grave cloth is undisputed. It therefore makes sense to seek a simile originating from this period in order to be able to say: "Look, the cloth was forged shortly before its first exhibition."

A group of French Catholic traditionalists, who call themselves "Catholic Counter-Reformation of the 20th Century" were the first who investigated the circumstances and published their findings in 1991.[76] They found out that Tite had sent a letter dated from 12-02-1988 to the Director of the Radiocarbon Laboratory at the University of Lyon, Jacques Evin, in which he asked for help in obtaining a suitable piece of fabric. Tite initially denied that he had written it, but when the letter was finally published, he had to admit his authorship[77]:

Dear Dr. Evin,

...I would certainly very much welcome any assistance that you can give in obtaining a medieval control sample, which is as similar as possible in terms of weave and colour as the Shroud, since at present, I am not certain whether the British Museum will be able to provide such a sample...

1: The total sample would need to be 6 sq. cms, (i.e. about 120 mg)

2: The material of the sample should be linen. I enclose a photocopy of some photographs which give some indication of the weave of the Shroud.

3: We are looking for a sample which dates from the 13th or the 14th century A.D., preferably the latter.

4: The historical precision should obviously be as good as possible, but one would certainly consider samples with an age range of fifty to a hundred years.

---

76 www.ewtn.com/library/ISSUES/STURP.TXT
77 www.ewtn.com/catholicism/library/great-holy-shroud-dating-fraud-of-1988-11057

5: There is no need for the sample to come from a well known piece of textile. ...

Yours Sincerely, Signed: M. S. Tite.

Ask yourself, dear reader, why should be such an exact date be necessary for a blank test? This would indeed complicate the search unnecessarily. If you follow the paper in Nature , none of the blank samples had the herringbone pattern of the shroud. Why go to so much trouble in obtaining this piece?

It seems that Evin could not provide the desired piece, because it is reported that Tite obtained a piece of fabric dating from the 14th century, from the Victoria and Albert Museum (London) - a sample which is not mentioned in the Nature article.[78]

Curiously, however, Evin did indeed find a piece of cloth (a cope of St. Ludwig, dated 1296/97), which he wanted to personally hand over to Tite in Turin, as fibers in a bag, immediately before the packing of the blanks was to start. But Tite refused to accept the bag, which he himself had requested. In the end, however, the samples were accepted and sent to the institutes as the fourth sample.

The determined age of this sample is almost identical to the age which was determined for the Shroud sample: Shroud: 1260 - 1390, Cope: 1263 - 1283 - The large uncertainty interval noted for the "shroud" of 130 years is remarkable, for the cope only 20 years are stated.

For further details, I refer to the books already cited, as well as the YouTube video : „The Shroud of Turin 1988 Carbon Dating: Triumph or Travesty?" www.youtube.com/watch?v=JBDuKZSgDSI

---

78 http://www.shroud.com/pdfs/vanhels6.pdf

The attitude of the Catholic Church

The retired pastor Karl Herbst asked in writing the then Cardinal Ratzinger, Riggi and Testore for clarification of specific issues. Ratzinger referred to Monsignor Giulio Ricci; Ricci however, did not react to Herbst's letter that followed. Riggi and Testore responded, but as soon as it went to the clarification of the main facts, they referred to "Vatican authorities": "*For more details ... you need to turn on now to the ecclesiastical authority, and to those in charge of the monitoring, who worked on that day.*"[79] Honest concern for clarification looks different.

The Catholic Church refuses to provide another cloth sample for carbon 14 testing. The cardinal of Turin even demanded the return of previously removed pieces that have long circulated in private:"*The Holy See permits no one possession or further use of such samples*".[80] Only the one medieval age determination of 1988 is supposed to be valid. Although the Shroud was seen by millions of people during its last exhibition in Turin in 2000 and is considered the most important relic of Christendom, the Catholic Church holds it in a mysterious gray zone. A popular German newspaper in August 2002 stated:

Since the C-14 tests in the year 1988 have hardened the hypothesis that the "miraculous" image of Christ on the almost four-and-a-half-meter-long linen cloth is an artifact from the 13th century, a slow and very careful distancing process has been carried out by the Church. The term, "sacra sindone" (holy shroud) is no longer used, while the worship of the Shroud by pilgrims to Turin is endured but no longer encouraged.[81]

Freely conducted international research on the Shroud has not been possible for more than twenty years. In 1984 the STURP group submitted a request, which came to nothing. In 1990 there was a "call for papers" by the Vatican, but "*six years later Cardinal Saldarini asked the researchers "to be patient, until a clear and systematically planned research project has been drafted"' This was the last time that anyone ever heard of it.*"[82]

In a letter to me, Poletto [the present Cardinal of Turin] mentioned that the research suggestions would still be accepted up to the end of

---

79 Herbst p. 174, Riggi's answering letter
80 Statement of the Cardinal of Turin, Saldarini, in September 1995, Wilson, p. 426
81 Frankfurter Allgemeine Zeitung, August 13, 2002.
82 Meacham, 2005, p. 240.

2002. He explained further that these suggestions would be evaluated by
an international jury of scientists. . . . How would this jury be selected?
Who belongs to it?. . . There are no answers.[83]

Every attempt to once again allow neutral, international research on the Shroud, or even a new carbon 14 test, comes to nothing. The Shroud, which is actually an inheritance of all humanity, is unfortunately in the clutches of a small group of custodians in Turin. Things occur with the indulgence of the Vatican, for the Shroud is a top priority.

In the year 2002 the Shroud was "restored" by this group of people. This happened under the strictest secrecy and without a single outside expert being consulted. The so-called "Holland cloth," on top of which the Shroud was sewed after a fire in the sixteenth century, was removed, as were repair work that had been sewn in to fill out the holes created by the burns. Singed Shroud materials were likewise removed, and all areas affected by the fire were cleaned with a special vacuum cleaner. Afterwards, new sewing repairs were made, and a new backing cloth was sewn under the Shroud.

One can imagine the shock, outrage, and sadness that were expressed when the information about the "restoration" gradually leaked out. After all, much valuable information on the Shroud was thereby, and without necessity, irrevocably destroyed.[84]

In a major press conference after the restoration, Cardinal Polleto and others celebrated the work. "*All the speakers made constant reference to the "sullied", "dirty", "filthy" situation under the patches and on the corresponding inner side of the backing cloth...* [One speaker] *said: "It was filthy. I would not sleep in a sheet in this condition."*[85]

The Shroud was thus restored as one would restore a medieval painting: cleaning of the surface, replacement of the picture frame, and so on, all so that it would look nice and pretty. That at least seems to have been successfully achieved.

Public doubt is gradually growing about the accuracy of the 1988 carbon dating of the Shroud to the Middle Ages. The pressure on the custodians of the Shroud to allow new tests is increasing. In August 2003

---

83 Meacham, 2005, p. 238.

84 For example, see http://www.shroud.com/restored.htm

85 William Meacham was present in this event and reports in his book on page 189 in detail.

William Meacham wrote to Cardinal Poletto listing the precise reasons that made a new carbon 14 dating necessary and pleading with him to allow at least a small portion of the material removed during the restoration process to be used for a new carbon test - without success. To this day, every attempt to conduct a new C14 test has been blocked, and any independent research directly on the cloth has been made impossible.

The Church appears to be in a major dilemma. On the one hand, the cloth confirms the historicity of Jesus and documents the Passion reports down to the smallest detail. On the other hand, it seems to strip historical ground from the core dogma of traditional belief.

As history teaches with the collapse of communist ideology, those in power can delay necessary historical developments. But they cannot prevent this in the long term, because the truth always paves its way, even if it takes time. Is it conceivable that the church will face the inevitable before it "comes too late and life punishes it", as Gorbachev once so aptly put it?

As the Church of Jesus Christ, it should be committed to the truth. Soon after the C14 results were announced, the church downgraded the cloth from a relic (something real) to an icon (a work of art or a fake). Pope Francis still speaks of an icon. It's strange: when various scientists traveled to Turin in the 1970s to examine the Shroud (STURP examination), most of them were skeptical. Dr. Rogers was convinced that the shroud would soon be exposed as a forgery.

For the Catholic Church, the cloth was at that time their most important relic. Most of the scientists went home impressed and convinced of the authenticity of the cloth. The top of the church, however, still sees it as a work of art to this day. The statement is: The cloth is a mystery, because it shows the traces of Christ's suffering in a clear and haunting way. But is it actually the real shroud of the historical Jesus? There are the results of the C14 test! We do not want to close ourselves off from scientific knowledge.

What Happened during and after the Crucifixion?

The punishment of crucifixion was an extremely humiliating and horrible torture, which often lasted for days until the victim finally died. It was, therefore, used above all as a deterrent to silence and force obedience in rebellious peoples. The victims were routinely nailed naked to their crosses.

The Gospels report that Jesus was nailed to the cross at about 9:00 a.m. and, at the latest, "gave up the ghost" at about 3:00 p.m. (the "ninth hour").

Joseph of Arimathea, a prominent member of the Council, who was himself waiting for the kingdom of God, went boldly to Pilate and asked for Jesus' body. Pilate was surprised to hear that he was already dead. Summoning the centurion, he asked him if Jesus had already died. When he learned from the centurion that it was so, he gave the body to Joseph. So Joseph bought some linen cloth, took down the body, wrapped it in the linen, and placed it in a tomb cut out of rock. Then he rolled a stone against the entrance of the tomb. (Mark 15:43–46)

A rapid death after only six hours in a crucifixion was something very unusual. The two other men crucified with Jesus had to have their legs broken in order to make them die quickly. Jesus was in the prime of his life and of strong physical constitution. He was, in regard to the flogging, not treated differently than other condemned men, who likewise had to endure such tortures.

During the Jewish War of AD 66–70, the historian Josephus Flavius found himself on a scouting expedition on behalf of the commander Titus. He writes:

When I returned, I saw many prisoners crucified and recognized three of them as my former associates. In my heart I was very sad about this and went with tears in my eyes to Titus and told him about it. And then he instantly gave the order to have them taken down and that they should be well treated, so that they would recover. Two of them unfortunately died while in the care of doctors, while the third did recover.[86]

Thus there were cases in which the crucified survived. But how is it possible that Jesus was only apparently dead and that those involved in the crucifixion, especially the Roman execution squad, could be so deceived?

---

86 Quoted in Gruber and Kersten, p. 59.

One can only speculate about this.

A jar of wine vinegar was there, so they soaked a sponge in it, put the sponge on a stalk of the hyssop plant, and lifted it to Jesus' lips. When he had received the drink, Jesus said, "It is finished." With that, he bowed his head and gave up his spirit. (John 19:29–30)

Jesus lost consciousness immediately after he drank some of the liquid. Is it possible that this vessel was not there by coincidence and perhaps held a strong narcotic substance? The soporific effects of opiates and other herbs were well known at the time.

But when they came to Jesus and found that he was already dead, they did not break his legs. Instead, one of the soldiers pierced Jesus' side with a spear, bringing a sudden flow of blood and water. (John 19:33–34)

How could the rest of the story have run? Two men, about whom later nothing is heard, concerned themselves with Jesus, believed by others to be dead. They were Nicodemus and Joseph of Arimathea. Both were re-spected citizens and councilors. Joseph was a rich merchant who had shortly before obtained a tomb for himself in the immediate vicinity of the crucifixion. Was this a coincidence? Everything had to happen quickly because the Sabbath was approaching, and with it all burial preparations had to cease. Joseph had a valuable shroud, Nicodemus a large quantity of myrrh and aloes. It appears odd but the burial must have occurred rather according to medical purposes than religious rules. The body was not washed, which helped to prevent further blood loss. The healing power of aloe and myrrh was well known in the ancient world. Did the two men know or suspect that Jesus was still alive? Was the burial only a ruse that had to be carried out in order to prevent Jesus from being executed a second time? If the truth had come out, then it would have cost the centurion and all the others who had saved the life of Jesus their own lives. The laws of Rome would have demanded it.

The tomb lay in the immediate area, only a few dozen meters distant from Golgotha.[87] Upon the body flowers were strewn. Upon the eyes two coins were laid. Everyone watching would have thought that a dead man was being buried. The Shroud was wrapped over the body, and a stone was rolled in front of the tomb's entrance.

What then occurred can be understood from reading the Gospel of Peter, which has been dated to AD 100–150. It reports the following:

---

87 Both Golgotha and the tomb of Jesus are found in the Church of the Holy Sepulchre in Jerusalem.

But during the night before the Lord's day dawned, as the soldiers were keeping guard two by two in every watch, there came a great sound in the sky, and they saw the heavens opened and two men descend shining with a great light, and they drew near to the tomb. The stone which had been set on the door rolled away by itself and moved to one side, and the tomb was opened and both of the young men went in.

Now when these soldiers saw that, they woke up the centurion and the elders (for they also were there keeping watch). While they were yet telling them the things which they had seen, they saw three men come out of the tomb, **two of them sustaining the other one,** *and a cross following after them.*[88]

If one leaves aside the ornate miracles, one reads that two men entered the tomb and three men came out, whereby the two men supported the third man. Why was this written? A supernaturally resurrected man needs no such support. Many interpreters of scripture today are of the view that a Gospel passage that does not agree with the ruling dogmas can rather be considered authentic because many texts that diverged from the evolving views were later rewritten or destroyed. Was this passage the reason why the Gospel of Peter was not included in the Canon of the New Testament, because it did not fit with the dogma of a supernatural resurrection?

In the Gospel of John it is further reported:

"Early on the first day of the week, while it was still dark, Mary Magdalene went to the tomb and saw that the stone had been removed from the entrance. So she came running to Simon Peter and the other disciple, the one Jesus loved, and said, 'They have taken the Lord out of the tomb, and we don't know where they have put him!'

So Peter and the other disciple started for the tomb. Both were running, but the other disciple outran Peter and reached the tomb first. He bent over and looked in at the strips of linen lying there but did not go in. Then Simon Peter, who was behind him, arrived and went into the tomb. He saw the strips of linen lying there, as well as the burial cloth that had been around Jesus' head. The cloth was folded up by itself, separate from the linen. Finally the other disciple, who had reached the tomb first, also went inside. He saw and believed. (John 20:1–8)

This running race was surely not forgotten by either of them for the rest of their lives. No wonder that John, when he either wrote this text himself

---

88 Compare: www.gospels.net/peter

or later told his experiences to his own disciples, could recall such detail so exactly. Much speaks for the conclusion that the Gospel of John represents the most historically exact mirroring of the passion and burial because its text comes from a direct eyewitness.

All the details speak for a natural course of events: the rolled-away stone (a resurrected man with a supernatural body who can walk through walls needs no stone rolled away from his tomb entrance), the folded cloths (why should a resurrected man bother to fold cloths?). It seems more plausible to assume that there were helpers who had cleaned up the tomb shortly before the disciples arrived.

Who were the mysterious men who the Gospels describe as young men or angels in white robes? Does the trail lead to the Essenes, who wore such white robes?

The helpers in the background were in mortal danger. Had their work become known, the Romans would have crucified them immediately and Jesus with them. The young man (or men) in the tomb could not have belonged to the immediate circle of the disciples, otherwise the women would have recognized him.

Was Nicodemus was the. Nothing will be reported about him later? He was a disciple of Jesus "in secret" and a member of the high council. Organizing an honorable funeral for someone who had been executed was very brave. Was he the man behind the scenes organizing the rescue of Jesus?

While they [the Emmaus desciples] *were still talking about this, Jesus himself stood among them and said to them, "Peace be with you."*

They were startled and frightened, thinking they saw a ghost. He said to them, "Why are you troubled, and why do doubts rise in your minds? Look at my hands and my feet. It is I myself! Touch me and see; a ghost does not have flesh and bones, as you see I have."

When he had said this, he showed them his hands and feet. And while they still did not believe it because of joy and amazement, he asked them, "Do you have anything here to eat?" They gave him a piece of broiled fish, and he took it and ate it in their presence."[89]

One can only guess what emotional roller coaster the disciples went through. First they had to accept the death of Jesus. Now he was suddenly standing before them in person. No wonder that at first they believed they were seeing a ghost and were afraid. But obviously it was important for

89 Lk 24:36-43

Jesus to convince the disciples that it was himself, in his natural body, who stood before them. This becomes very clear in the Gospel of John:

"Now Thomas, one of the Twelve, was not with the disciples when Jesus came. So the other disciples told him, "We have seen the Lord!" But he said to them, "Unless I see the nail marks in his hands and put my finger where the nails were, and put my hand into his side, I will not believe." A week later his disciples were in the house again, and Thomas was with them. Though the doors were locked, Jesus came and stood among them and said, "Peace be with you!" Then he said to Thomas, "Put your finger here; see my hands. Reach out your hand and put it into my side. Stop doubting and believe." Thomas said to him, "My Lord and my God!"[90]

It was not an apparition, it was Jesus himself who could be touched. Why should someone who knew the story behind tell the truth when it was rumored that Jesus was resurrected? As long as a supernatural process is assumed, the helpers were off the hook. Pilate was not interested in an investigation. An unsuccessful crucifixion as a result of an examination would have been an embarrassment for him and the Roman occupying power. He probably didn't feel like poking around in this case, as the trial had already disgusted him. He wanted to let Jesus go and have the rebel Barabbas executed. Sometimes it is wise to let things go.

Had "Jesus" been a supernatural phenomenon, he would have been invulnerable and could have appeared in public without any problems. That this did not happen suggests that he belonged to the mortals even after his (natural) resurrection. According to the Islamic view, Jesus did not die on the cross. This belief is mainly based on Sura 4 in the Koran:

And about their speech: "We have killed the Messiah, Jesus, the son of Mary, the messenger of Allah." Yet they neither struck him dead nor let him die on the cross, but rather it only appeared to them so; and those who disagree in this matter are probably in doubt about it; they have no (certain) information of it, but rather believe only a suspicion; and they have no certainty of it. (Sura 4:157–58)

With that, it was to be shown to the Jews that God would frustrate their hostile intentions toward Mohammed just as he had theirs toward Jesus.

---

90 Joh 20:24-28

The belief that Jesus had a long life and wandered after the crucifixion as far as Kashmir was spread by the Islamic Ahmadiya movement:

His tomb is venerated in Srinagar.[91] If Jesus did not die shortly after saying goodbye to his disciples, it seems likely that he left the Roman Empire. Anyone would have immediately identified him as crucified by his scars. He would probably have been crucified again. His disciples would have been in great danger too. The "Ascension" was the narrative counterpart to the supernatural resurrection. During the time in between, Jesus must have been in a supernatural intermediate world most of the time. So it wouldn't have needed any helpers to look for. Who could have guessed at that time which impact the life of Yeshua, as he was called by his friends, would have in history?

---

91 en.wikipedia.org/wiki/Jesus_in_Ahmadiyya_Islam

Christian Religion versus Religion of Jesus

Put not your faith in illusions. They will fail you. Put all your faith in the
Love of God within you; eternal, changeless and forever unfailing.

A Course in Miracles

The Christian world is changing. Much does not fit into today's thinking
anymore. It is permissible, even en vogue, to question "truths" that have
been considered irrefutable for many centuries. The book by Prof. Johannes Fried: "Kein Tod auf Golgatha: Auf der Suche nach dem über-
lebenden Jesus" (No Death on Golgotha: In Search of the Surviving Jesus") made it into Bestseller lists.

The thing is delicate: a Jesus whose body is decaying in the grave cannot
be seen by 500 people. So what happened in this scenario: hallucinations?
Psychologically speaking, these "encounters" would then be forms of denial of reality. The actual truth would have been so terrible for the disciples that in their desperation they would have fled into the comforting
idea of a resurrection, contrary to all reality. Today you might be diag-
nosed with a psychotic disorder.

There is a lot to suggest that a resurrection actually took place. The only
question is: did it happen within the laws of nature or not? If Jesus was
really biologically dead and the encounters actually took place after the
crucifixion as presented in the Gospels, then there is obviously a conflict
between science and religion: something impossible in the sense of science is accepted as historical truth. You can of course believe that, but the
question is: Is this belief in miracles really necessary to be a Christian
and to believe in the love of God?

If the resurrection took place within the laws of nature, the matter is clear
from a dogmatic point of view: no death, no sacrificial death, no atone-
ment for our sins, no redemption of humanity. Paul made it very clear: "If
Christ has not been raised, our preaching is useless and so is your faith."
(1 Cor. 15:14) Paul gambled high when he linked the redemption of
mankind to a supernatural resurrection. But Paul was not Jesus. Jesus

didn't even know him personally. Had he found out about his letters - perhaps in India - he would have been probably upset. He would have found his behavior as an apostle as presumptuous. According to Paul 'conviction, Jesus bought the forgiveness of sins through his suffering on the cross for everyone who believes in him in this way. But Jesus himself refused the sacrifices in the temple. Sacrifice is not necessary, God is love! The very idea that one can or must "buy" something from love is absurd. One cannot get anything from love through suffering, money, or good works. Jesus quoted the Old Testament to illustrated what he thinks about sacrifices (Hosea 6: 6): "I desire mercy, not sacrifice."

In a sense, Jesus sacrificed himself. But not to appease a higher power or to bring about reconciliation. Because God does not need to be reconciled. Love does not condemn. Therefore she does not need to forgive either. What profit should suffering create?

Jesus could have fled in time and could have written valuable books about the kingdom of God abroad, perhaps in the kingdom of King Abgar. But what would he have proven by that? That you can't really rely on God. That death is stronger than life, fear stronger than love. He has always remained in love - even on the cross. In doing so, he overcame sin, death, and fear. For himself and for us too. That could be a timelessly modern interpretation of the crucifixion that is consistent with the religion of Jesus.

That he survived the crucifixion was an unpredictable "bonus". In my eyes, his "resurrection" testifies to an unconditional will to live. On the cross he could have returned to his "Heavenly Father". But he chose to stay in his body and accomplish his mission. What a human! He was verily the Son of God. But he also said that this identity applies to all of us. Because all people are children of God and are created in his image.

Literature

Resurrection believed as survival in general:
Johannes Fried, Kein Tod auf Golgatha: Auf der Suche nach dem über-
lebenden Jesus, 2019
Franz Alt, Die außergewöhnlichste Liebe aller Zeiten, 2021

Turin Shroud

**Standard works, the resurrection usually believed to be a supernatu-
ral event**
Werner Bulst, Das Turiner Grabtuch: Zugang zum historischen Jesus,
1978
Werner Bulst, Betrug am Grabtuch, 1990
Ian Wilson, Das Turiner Grabtuch: Die Wahrheit, 1999
William Meacham, The Rape of the Shroud, 2005
Mary & Alan Whanger, The Shroud of Turin: An Adventure of Discov-
ery, 1998
Philip E. Dayvault, The Keramion – Lost and Found, 2016
Frederick T. Zugibe, The Crucifixion of Jesus: A Forensic Inquiry, 2005

Raymond N. Rogers, A Chemist's Perspective On The Shroud of Turin,
2011
A highly recommended book, available from www.lulu.com

Thesis: Survival of the Crucifixion
Elmar R. Gruber und Holger Kersten, Jesus starb nicht am Kreuz: Die
Botschaft des Turiner Grabtuchs, 1998
Gerhard Kunke, Rom und das Grabtuch: Skandal in Turin, 2004
Karl Herbst, Kriminalfall Golgatha, 1992
Rodney Hoare, The Turin Shroud is Genuine,1994

Other books in the series

Read Volume 2 of the New Light on Jesus series: In Search of the "Real God" - Beyond Pauline Christianity (Ebook)

Find out: How the Christian religion came into being in the first centuries and what major errors crept into this process.

Possible approaches to the "Real God" The answer is in the religion of Jesus, beyond the Christian religion.

As a supplement to this non-fiction book, a novel is available from the same author (in German):

Die Memoiren des Judas Iskariot

Due to the intervention of the Vatican, ancient scrolls, which were discovered in 1910 by Prof. von Engelthal near Qumran, remained under lock and key for a long time. Judas tells about his life with Jeshua: childhood, discipleship, alienation, betrayal, and their escapes to Kashmir.

When they learn from Paul that the crucifixion is interpreted as an atoning death, Judas travels back to Judea. However, his words go unheard. So he decides to write down his true story.

Who could better write a biography of Jesus than his disciple, greatest critic, traitor and friend, Judas. In his memoirs he describes his eventful life with Jeshua, his own inner processes from an enthusiastic follower to a disappointed traitor who wants to kill himself. He describes how his master's love reached him at the last moment and how a second life was given to both of them.

Photo credits

No	Name	Link	Original	Autor	License	Comment
0	Cover: Ressurection of Christ			Romolo Tavani	Istock	fitted
1	General view of the shroud	de.wikipedia.org/wiki/Turiner_Grabtuch#/media/Datei:Shroudofturin.jpg		Giuseppe Enrie 1931	Ⓒ	
2	Delivery in Constantinople	en.wikipedia.org/wiki/History_of_the_Shroud_of_Turin#/media/File:Surrender_of_the_Mandylion_to_the_Byzantines.jpg	Manuscript of the Skylitzes (Madrid)	Cplakidas	Ⓒ	
3	King Abgar with the "Edessa image"	commons.wikimedia.org/wiki/File:Abgarwithimageofedessa10thcentury.jpg	St. Catherine's Monastery	St. Catherine's	Ⓒ	
4	Santa Costanza mosaic	https://commons.wikimedia.org/wiki/File:Traditio_Legis_mosaic_-_Santa_Costanza_-_Rome_2016.jpg?uselang=de	Santa Costanza Church Rome	© José Luiz Bernardes Ribeiro	CC BY-SA 4.0	
5	Jesus as a good shepherd	https://de.wikipedia.org/wiki/Datei:Good_shepherd_02.jpg	Catacomb of St. Callistus		Ⓒ	fitted
6	Fresco Marcellinus and Paulus	commons.wikimedia.org/wiki/File:%C2%B7_Jes%C3%BAs_Cristo_flanqueado_por_San_Pedro_y_San_Pablo_%C2%B7_Catacumbas_de_los_Santos_Pedro_y_Marcelino,_Roma,_s._IV_d._JC._%C2%B7.jpg	Catacombs Peter and Paul Rome		Ⓒ	fitted
7	Santa Pudenziana mosaic	https://commons.wikimedia.org/wiki/File:Apsis_mosaic,_Santa_Pudenziana,_Rome_W2.JPG	Santa Pudenziana Church	Welleschik	CC BY-SA 3.0	fitted
8	Mandylion as a field standard		Imperial Museum London		Ⓒ	
9	Ravenna before 544	de.wikipedia.org/wiki/San_Vitale#/media/Datei:Ravenna_Basilica_of_San_Vitale_mosaic_Christ2.jpg	San Vitale Ravenna	Ruge	CC BY-SA 4.0	fitted
10	Ravenna after 544	commons.wikimedia.org/wiki/Category:Interior_of_San_Vitale_(Ravenna)?uselang=de#/media/File:Intrados_with_Christ_and_Martyrs_Basilica_of_San_Vitale_Ravenna_(6098661558).jpg	San Vitale Ravenna	Sharon Mollerus	CC BY-SA 2.0	fitted
11	Jesus Pantocrator	de.wikipedia.org/wiki/Pantokrator#/media/Datei:Spas_vsederzhitel_sinay.jpg	Catherine's Monastery	St. Catherine's	Ⓒ	processed
12	Justinian coin	commons.wikimedia.org/wiki/File:Suaire_de_Turin_et_monnaie_or_Byzantine_Empereur_Justinien_VIIIeme_siecle.jpg		Afprz	Ⓒ	
13	Gero cross	en.wikipedia.org/wiki/History_of_the_Shroud_of_Turin#/media/File:Shroud_of_Lirey_Pilgrim_Badge.jpg	Cologne cathedral	Elke Wetzig	CC BY-SA 3.0	
14	Pilgrim medal	hen.wikipedia.org/wiki/History_of_the_Shroud_of_Turin#/media/File:Shroud_of_Lirey_Pilgrim_Badge.jpg		Arthur Forgeais	Ⓒ	
15	Shroud: back of the body	de.wikipedia.org/wiki/Turiner_Grabtuch#/media/Datei:Shroudofturin.jpg		Giuseppe Enrie 1931	Ⓒ	
16	Painting Giovanni Battista	en.wikipedia.org/wiki/History_of_the_Shroud_of_Turin#/media/File:OntstaanLijkwade_GiovanniBattista.png	Galleria Sabauda Turin		Ⓒ	

Ⓒ = Public domain